SHE'S LIKED THE GIRLS BEST

M000032334

"Liberating freshness . . . her tone is light and her sensibility startling." —*The Boston Globe*

"Claudia Allen, a gay Chicago playwright with a growing national reputation, here skillfully blends campy nostalgia with contemporary gay political attitudes. . . . Allen's riotous and often ribald one-liners come with rapid-fire regularity." —*Bay Windows*

"Allen's dialogue is consistently entertaining, often brilliantly funny, at times reminiscent of Lanford Wilson in its smooth realism and subtlety. Allen has a fine ear, and her use of the everyday miracle of unexpectedly intelligent small-talk through which strong feelings and the deeper soundings of life are revealed, shows a solid grasp of the possibilities at the heart of the drama." —*Windy City Times*

"Combining humor and pathos with in-depth characterization of its central characters, *Hannah Free* emerges as a full-blown multi-layered story. . . . shows a mature lesbian playwright at the top of her craft." —*Chicago Reader*

ALSO BY CLAUDIA ALLEN

PUBLISHED PLAYS

Movie Queens (Chicago Plays Edition)

The Long Awaited (Chicago Plays Edition)

Still Waters (in *Plays by Women: One Hundred Years of Feminism in American Drama*, Carol Cyganowski, editor)

Ripe Conditions (Dramatic Publishing)

Winter (Dramatic Publishing)

AVAILABLE FROM THE AUTHOR

Deed of Trust

Dutch Love

The Freedom Rider

The Gays of Our Lives

Just Desserts

The Last of Bilky Ciliax

The Return of Christmas

Reunion (the glass ceiling play)

They Even Got the Rienzi

The Usher

SHE'S ALWAYS LIKED THE GIRLS BEST

lesbian plays

Roomers

Raincheck

Hannah Free

Movie Queens

Claudia Allen

Third Side Press

Chicago

CAUTION

Professionals and amateurs take heed: The plays in *She's Always Liked the
Girls Best* are fully protected under the copyright laws of the United States
of America and all countries of the Berne and Universal Copyright
Conventions. All rights, including professional, amateur, motion picture,
recitation, lecturing, public reading, radio and television broadcasting and
all other rights of public performance of any nature and rights of
translation are reserved. Any requests for the right to perform *Roomers*,
Raincheck, or *Hannah Free* in any manner whatsoever should be addressed
to Claudia Allen, c/o Third Side Press, 2250 W. Farragut, Chicago, IL
60625-1802, voice 312/271-3029, fax 312/271-0459; for rights to *Movie
Queens*, contact Chicago Plays, Inc., 2632 N. Lincoln, Chicago, IL 60614,
voice 312/348-4658, fax 312/348-5561.

ACKNOWLEDGMENT

Movie Queens is available in a script edition from Chicago Plays, Inc., 2632
N. Lincoln Ave., Chicago, IL 60614. Third Side Press thanks them for their
cooperation with the production of this edition of the play.

Library of Congress Cataloging-in-Publication Data
Allen, Claudia, 1954–
    She's always liked the girls best : lesbian plays / by Claudia
Allen. — 1st ed.
      p.   cm.
    Includes bibliographical references.
    Contents: Roomers — Raincheck — Hannah Free — Movie queens.
    ISBN 1-879427-11-7 :
    1. Lesbians—Drama.   I. Title.
PS3551.L39215S47   1992
812'.54—dc20   92-44359
                                  CIP

Cover photograph copyright © 1993 by Roger Lewin/Jennifer Girard Studios
Book design and production by Midge Stocker
  Text set 10.5/12 Century Schoolbook
Printed with soy-based ink on recycled, acid-free paper
  in the United States of America.

Third Side Press
2250 W. Farragut
Chicago, IL 60625-1802

First edition, February 1993

Second printing, February 1995
10 9 8 7 6 5 4 3 2

To Kay, with love

CONTENTS

FOREWORD

I first met Claudia Allen in Chicago in 1989 when she agreed to visit my DePaul University graduate class on Women Dramatists. *The Long Awaited*—later to win the Joseph Jefferson award for Outstanding New Work—was playing at Victory Gardens Theater. *Still Waters*—her second Jeff prizewinner—was awaiting a staged reading at Victory Gardens.

Claudia Allen had been a presence in Chicago and national theater before the Jeffs (and big audiences) found her in 1989. *Movie Queens*, printed here in its full two acts and twenty-eight scenes, was first seen as a one-act in New York in 1986. In the 1987 Great Chicago Playwrights Expo, Allen's *They Even Got the Rienzi* was one of fourteen plays, one of only two by women, chosen from more than five-hundred submissions. *The Rienzi* (a building that was demolished), one of Allen's earliest Chicago plays, focused on the telling combination of architectural preservation and urban politics and economics. Through numerous productions in Chicago and across the U.S., staged readings of new work and work-in-progress, teleplays (e.g., *Deer Season),* and radio plays, ever more various theater audiences have had the opportunity to experience the range of Claudia Allen's work.

Claudia Allen's importance in the realm of lesbian theater is clear in the plays collected here, as well as in her riotously comic and technically innovative lesbian and gay "soap opera," *The Gays of Our Lives*. Conceived by Lee Roy Rogers and Claudia Allen and written by Allen, *Gays* premiered in Fall 1991 at Chicago's Zebra Crossing Theatre as three individual episodes: "Chicken of the Sea," "The Dragon Lady and the Big Gaysha," and "Women In and Behind Bars." Together, these episodes became *The Gays of Our Lives, the Play*, produced first at Zebra Crossing and then in Portland and Los Angeles.

Those of us who read and teach drama have long awaited more of Allen's plays, in print as well as in production. Here

Third Side Press publisher Midge Stocker begins to answer that desire, with the first all-Claudia Allen anthology.

Three of the plays included in this collection appear in print for the first time. Two—*Raincheck and Roomers*—date from the mid-1980s, during Allen's prolific early years as a playwright. *Movie Queens* in the present version premiered in 1990 at Chicago's Zebra Crossing Theatre. *Hannah Free* premiered in 1992 at Chicago's Bailiwick Repertory Gay & Lesbian Theatre Festival.

Certain themes recur throughout these plays of love and of love hidden or postponed. The closet's hiding and pretending—and the pain it brings to the lover who's hidden—is central to *Hannah Free* and to *Movie Queens*. While *Hannah*'s Hannah leaves the "same old" of the restrictive Michigan town and leaves Rachel, Hannah—like Meg in *Movie Queens*—returns again and again to her closeted lover, returning both for love and to give voice to the courage of knowing and being oneself. Love and courage are examined again and again in these plays. Characters—and audiences—are asked to see the difference between needing and wanting; to feel the pain of the lover who "just didn't mean enough" for her partner to overcome social convention and prejudice or to take the risk of loving.

These themes are made all the more powerful because of Allen's sympathetic, even celebratory, treatment of age and aging. Her characters want to grow old together, to sit on the porch and hold hands, to be themselves and enjoy themselves. Allen's extensions through time bring lovers and audiences both to resolutions that would be unavailable if we saw love as the province of the young and if we saw relationships as potentially too damaged to leave a "raincheck" for later connection. Allen and her characters don't give up, and they gain courage and self-knowledge as they age.

In addition to their woman-centered worlds and strong women characters, these Claudia Allen plays share other characteristic features of women's drama. The character who is in the play but never on the stage—a technique many date from Susan Glaspell's groundbreaking *Trifles* (1916)—is fundamental to explaining Adele's behavior in *Movie Queens* (as she reacts to the threats of the sleazy studio head). The action of *Raincheck* starts when Betsy's leaving Gwen and Thema's leaving Rule quite literally set the stage for Grandma Pansy to ask Gwen, "Did you hear about Thema and Rule?" We hear quite a bit about Thema and Rule and about a younger Thema and a pre-Betsy Gwen, yet both Rule and Betsy are noticeably absent from the stage as Thema and Gwen rediscover their past and their unused raincheck.

The real bad-guys (Rule in *Raincheck*, the studio head in *Movie Queens*, Maynard and the abusive small town boys in *Roomers*) are missing from Allen's stage. The sense of women's space, a dramatic space for self-definition, is strongly articulated by distinctions between those who are invited into the space and interlopers who must be ousted from it. Clearing the porch in *Roomers*, clearing Hannah's and then Rachel's room in *Hannah Free*, ousting Sydney from the dressing room in *Movie Queens*—all these acts of reclaiming space, of refusing others' definitions of and impositions on the self, are very satisfying assertions.

The space that is claimed—and reclaimed—is, as in many women's plays, often a limited domestic space. Sharing the positive values of women's spaces, Allen's particular settings also carry some of the usual associations of enclosure and entrapment. Hannah of *Hannah Free* certainly feels bound by her capture in the nursing home, as Pansy and Flora of *Raincheck* are bound by their age and infirmities. The small towns and even the circumscribed world of Hollywood can be narrow, confining, entrapping worlds. But Allen, especially in the smalltown plays, does a new take on spatial and geographic limitation.

In setting many of her dramas in the smalltown Michigan she knows so well, Claudia Allen both participates in and rings changes on the American dramatic tradition of the small town. As Ima Honaker Herron notes in *The Small Town in American Drama* (Dallas: Southern Methodist University Press, 1969), "Since the late eighteenth century this feeling for community, or interrelationship, has been portrayed so frequently in native plays interpreting the small town and its folk. . . . a tendency toward introspection, longing for community" (vii). Like so many American playwrights before her, Allen sees the small town not only as offering community but also as harboring small-minded viciousness and intolerance. With the smalltown's eulogy read so many times in twentieth-century American drama, we might expect lesbian plays of the 1980s and 1990s to find little range and life in such circumscribed spaces and ideas.

Allen's limited spaces and small towns, her worlds of widows and orphans, engender always—and strongly—woman-defined spaces of community and continuity and a variety of possibilities for love. With women characters across generations reinforcing the importance of caring and love, we could expect—and even hope—that Allen is offering us a setting in which to celebrate love between women. Finally, though Allen is sympathetic to the small town, she is a realist.

Her characters know and speak (as they do in *Raincheck*) of the "little privacy" included in the "thrills of living in a small town." Gwen can't imagine "why I wanted to stay here so bad I'd lose her to do it" when Betsy leaves to find "some place where she could blend in." So why set lesbian love stories in the restrictive atmosphere of provincial small towns? Why use the sardonic humor and wisdom of older women as a foil for both acceptance and rejection? Why develop the contrast of wandering and looking against the lover who must never, who will never, leave home? What Allen gets from her smalltown settings is enormous resonance against the eternal actions of coming out, coping with homophobia, finding self, and finding love. The smalltown locations and the charming, tentative love scenes Allen sets there highlight questions of individual courage and caring rather than of place alone. The characters who stay and those who return all eventually claim space, both dramatic and personal.

The ironies available in this naturalistically presented world, and the humor available in resistance, allow us to understand both characters' literal realities and their visions of a more reasonable society. With characters who move outside and through the realistic central actions (the Old Man in *Hannah Free*, Flora in *Raincheck*, Maynard in *Roomers*) introducing elements of the violent and bizarre, both representation of self and location in time become increasingly problematized. As characters reconstruct and recover their past and present, Allen's stage moves beyond literal naturalism to representations of memory, of love lost and reclaimed that move us far beyond the living room, the nursing home, the rooming-house porch, or even the backstage dressing room. The world is finally one of rather complex understanding, for those who can, around central realistic core dramas of love, for those who will.

Carol Klimick Cyganowski,
Associate Professor of English &
Director, Women's Studies Program
DePaul University, Chicago

Acknowledgments

First and foremost, I want to thank Midge Stocker for publishing this anthology of my lesbian plays. It was her idea and her hard work that made it happen.

These plays cover a number of years in my writing career, so I want to thank all the actors and directors involved in all the many readings and productions.

Specifically, I'd like to thank the now-defunct Stonewall Repertory in New York City for deciding to produce the one-act version of *Movie Queens*, because that production led to others and eventually to this full-length version which premiered at Zebra Crossing Theatre in Chicago in a wonderful production directed by Marlene Zuccaro. Thanks to Marlene and Zebra Crossing.

Thank you, Laurie Attea, for directing the first production of *Hannah Free* and making me appreciate what I wrote. And thank you, Cherise and Pat and everyone at the Portland Women's Theatre Company, for the second production of *Hannah* and for producing so many years of terrific women's theater.

Roomers and *Raincheck* have not yet been fully produced,[*] but all sorts of wonderful people have read these parts, including and especially Barbara June Patterson, Nancy Lollar, Meg Thalken, and Lee Guthrie. And thank you to Ann and Linda at Women & Children First for hosting so many of the readings.

I am a Playwright-in-Residence at Victory Gardens Theater in Chicago, and I want to thank my longtime friend and director there, Sandy Shinner, for her insights into these plays and her

---

[*] As of the second printing of this book, all of the plays had been fully produced.

encouragement. I also want to thank everyone at Victory Gardens for their support of new plays.

Paula Berg, Theresa Swedo, Diana Waller Suchoff, Donna O'Hara, Gail Altenburg, Carol Cyganowski, and Karen Lee Osborne—I'm so lucky to have such wonderful women in my life.

Finally, I thank my teachers and my students, my friends and my parents, Kay and our cats. You've all been very patient with me, especially the cats.

ROOMERS

Cast of Characters

Ida

June

Letty

Dinah

Mary Ann

Ed

Ernest

Setting

A roominghouse porch in smalltown Michigan in the 1980s.

Summary

Roomers is about mothers and daughters, relationships and strangers, and strange relationships that no longer seem so strange. In the course of the play, Letty, the teenaged daughter of the house comes to realize she has more than just a crush on a young woman visitor.

Author's Note

Roomers is a very personal exploration of my very ambiguous feelings about growing up in smalltown America, especially growing up fat and gay in smalltown America.

Scene 1

(The porch of a smalltown roominghouse. There is a round, metal ROOMS sign freestanding at the corner of the porch. It is early summer. There is a porch swing; assorted, mismatched chairs, a rocker among them; a pot or two of geraniums, petunias. Ida is sitting on the porch with June.)

JUNE I love to sit.

IDA I don't know how anybody can stand it who doesn't have a porch.

JUNE When I lived in Detroit, I felt lucky if I had a geranium in my window.

IDA I've never lived anywhere but here.

JUNE You ever wanted to?

IDA Oh, when I was younger. But cities scare me. I'd never know what bus to take.

JUNE You learn.

IDA When I graduated high school, my mother wanted me to go to business school in Lansing.

JUNE You didn't go?

IDA Oh I went, but I got so homesick I'd call her every night and cry. I think I lasted a week. City people must be so lonely.

JUNE It's like anywhere else. You get to know people.

IDA She said I never gave it a chance. I suppose I didn't.

JUNE Shows how different people are. When my Dinah started college she was in seventh heaven.

IDA She never did seem to like it here.

JUNE Well, it beats Detroit.

IDA I thought you liked Detroit.

JUNE I never said I liked Detroit. I just said you get used to it. Why in hell'd I move up here if I liked Detroit so much?

IDA You met Elta and she offered you a job.

JUNE   I already had a job. I moved outa Detroit before somebody shot me dead for my groceries. Say, did I remember to take my two o'clock pill?

IDA   You took it at three.

JUNE   Oh. Well, that's all right then.

IDA   Letty'll be home soon. Only one more week of school and she'll be out for the summer. Where does the time go?

(Brief lull.)

JUNE   It's been a quiet afternoon.

IDA   Quiet day.

JUNE   Nice though. *(Brief lull.)* How's your shoulder doin'?

IDA   Oh, it's fine. I think I just pulled it a little lifting that chair.

JUNE   Next time you wait for Ed.

IDA   I can lift a chair by myself, thank you very much.

JUNE   Next time you might pull somethin' vital.

IDA   June, I've seen you lift half a sofa.

JUNE   Well, you don't hear me complainin' I've pulled a muscle. It comes natural to my people. We're naturally stronger.

IDA   Oh, bull.

JUNE   It's true.

IDA   June, you are so full of it.

JUNE   How'd we pick all that cotton if we're not strong?

IDA   You never picked cotton in your life.

JUNE   Well, maybe not me personally . . .

IDA   Who then? Your mother? Your uncle? Your Aunt Jemima?

JUNE   I'm sure Somebody in my family picked cotton.

(Ida's daughter, Letty, enters with her schoolbooks. A boy calls from offstage.)

BOY'S VOICE Hey, lardass!

IDA *(To June.)* When I hear something like that it's lucky I
don't have a gun. *(To Letty.)* Hi, honey, how was school?

LETTY All right. *(She looks in the direction of the boy's voice.)*

JUNE Don't let that boy bother you, Letty. He's prob'ly just tryin'
to get your attention.

LETTY He did.

IDA *(Looking in the direction of the boy's voice.)* I used to date a
boy who looked a lot like him.

JUNE Lord honey, you got worse taste in men than I do.

IDA You know it might be his son. I heard he had a family after
he got out of prison.

LETTY I'm sure glad you never got married again.

JUNE Mary Ann still laid out in her room?

IDA Some women just have an awful time every month.

JUNE It's all in their head.

IDA It is not. At least mine's not.

JUNE You are so bad.

LETTY Is her creepy brother home yet?

IDA No, Maynard isn't home yet.

LETTY Good.

JUNE You know I lived in Detroit for twenty years, an' even I
think that boy's weird.

IDA Well, at least he leaves the seat down on the toilet.

LETTY I wish he'd talk to Ed. I almost fell in last night.

IDA We had one man here who used to pee in the sink. He
swore he didn't, but Letty wasn't tall enough at the time and
we didn't have a cat.

JUNE *(Speaking the knowledge of a long lifetime.)* Men don't care
where they pee.

LETTY Is Dinah around?

JUNE She went to the post office.

IDA Letty? While you're up . . .

LETTY Oh oh. *("While you're up" is obviously a ritual phrase between them.)*

IDA While you're up, would you mind making us some lemonade? June, you in the mood for lemonade?

JUNE Have I ever turned it down?

(Letty opens the screen door, preparing to trudge off to the kitchen.)

IDA How about bringin' us out a box of Girl Scout cookies while you're at it. Let's spoil our supper.

LETTY Anything else, madam queen?

IDA I'll let you know.

(Shaking her head, Letty exits.)

IDA She just likes to complain. She doesn't really mind.

JUNE They like to talk back. But you just look out after she's been to college. Then she'll Really think she knows it all.

IDA I'm gonna miss her a lot when she goes.

JUNE I gotta admit I was pretty lonesome the first year or two after Dinah left.

IDA It's too bad I'm allergic to cats. Maybe I could get a bird.

JUNE You can always adopt Mary Ann. She'd be easy to mother. She hasn't got the good sense God gave a rock.

IDA Poor Mary Ann. She's been up in their room all day. I should take her the heating pad.

JUNE I think it's a shame she and her brother can't afford two rooms; that they have to share that one room.

IDA *(Lifting one eyebrow.)* I don't think they want two rooms.

JUNE No!

IDA   I hear sounds. I wake up in the night and I hear sounds. It's not snoring I hear.

JUNE   Let's just hope they don't make a baby.

IDA   It'd be a pathetic sight.

JUNE   Pathetic. *(Brief pause.)* I gotta stop sleepin' so heavy. *(They laugh.)*

IDA   *(Craning.)* Here comes Ernest. He's after me about buyin' the house again.

JUNE   That little weasel thinks he's John D. Rockefeller.

IDA   Well, he does dream big. For this town.

JUNE   Dreamin' of buildin' the biggest Motel 6 in Michigan is not dreamin' big.

(Ernest enters.)

IDA   Hello, Ernest. Rest your feet.

ERNEST   Thank you I will. Hello, June.

JUNE   Mr. Bogg.

(Ernest sits.)

ERNEST   My angina's actin' up again.

IDA   It's the heat.

ERNEST   Blood pressure, too. I just checked it in the car.

(Letty enters through screen door carrying a tray. Her eyes narrow at the sight of Ernest.)

LETTY   I guess I should've made up another can.

IDA   Why don't you, honey? If you wouldn't mind. I'm sure Ernest would like a glass.

ERNEST   Has that got sugar in it?

LETTY   It's out of a can.

ERNEST   I try to avoid sugar.

IDA   Bring him a glass. He'll drink it.

(Letty, looking quite disgusted, exits.)

IDA   *(Offering the cookies to Ernest.)* Cookie? They're from the Girl Scouts. I always buy a case every year. They're my downfall.

ERNEST *(Taking one.)* Thank you. Just one. *(Nibbles.)*

JUNE   Remember that year somebody found razor blades in the Girl Scout cookies?

IDA   How could anybody do that to the Girl Scouts?

(Ernest disposes of the rest of his cookie by slipping it in his pocket or in a geranium. June and Ida watch him do it.)

IDA   Finished already?

ERNEST My wife used to love the peanut butter ones.

IDA   I remember. She used to order them from Letty.

ERNEST Do you know Anita's been dead four years come this Thanksgiving?

IDA   I always think of her when I'm making my turkey.

ERNEST I hope you stay away from the frozen ones.

IDA   Now Ernest, I'm sure I'm not gonna drop it on my foot and get gangrene like she did.

ERNEST Well, she didn't think she would either till she did it.

JUNE   *(Somewhat to herself.)* I always kinda wondered if she committed suicide.

ERNEST Who'd think I'd be alone at my age? Just me and my chain of Motel Sixes. I wouldn't have anything to live for if I didn't have my motels.

JUNE   Let's just hope the A-rabs don't shoot the price of gasoline back up so the tourist business goes to hell.

(Ernest looks sick.)

IDA   June, don't tease Ernest. He's not a well man.

ERNEST   Ida, have you given any more thought to my offer?

IDA   I like my house. I don't want you turning it into a parking lot.

ERNEST   Actually, this is where I thought I'd put the pool.

IDA   Ernest, what would I do without my house?

JUNE   Woman's got a right to keep her house if she wants to.

ERNEST   You can't block progress.

JUNE   You Aren't progress.

(Letty enters with a glass of lemonade for Ernest.)

LETTY   Here you go.

ERNEST   Thank you. Say, Letty?

LETTY   What?

ERNEST   Wouldn't you like to live in a nice new apartment, just you and your mother, without all these crazy roomers?

LETTY   Just me 'n Mom in an apartment, just the two of us?

ERNEST   Doesn't that sound nice?

LETTY   Are you kidding? We'd drive each other nuts.

IDA   That's my girl. *(But on second thought.)*   I don't know if we'd exactly drive each other nuts.

LETTY   *(Looking down the street.)*   I wish Dinah'd get back. Her visit's going so fast.

JUNE   They always do. She's barely here before she's gone.

ERNEST   Ida? *(He flaps about to get her attention.)*   Ida, if I can't buy this house from you, can I at least buy you dinner some night?

JUNE   The shit's gettin' deep now.

IDA   That would be nice, Ernest. You call me sometime.

ERNEST *(Takes a last sip of lemonade, rises.)* I hate to rush off, but I need to get home. I'm expecting a call from Saginaw. Have a nice evening, ladies.

IDA You, too.

LETTY Bye.

(Ernest steps off the porch and walks away. He exits, but the women can still see him from where they are.)

IDA Look. Watch him. He's walking so he won't step on any cracks.

JUNE Saginaw. You'd think it was a call from Paris, France.

LETTY Remember the summer he hit a black cat with his car?

IDA He wouldn't come out of his house all week. Poor Ernest. We shouldn't laugh.

JUNE I wanna know how you could tell that pompous little pissant you'd go out with him.

IDA He'll never call. He's too cheap.

LETTY Don't let her fool you, June. She'd dying for him to call. She's been in love with Ernest Bogg ever since they were little kids.

JUNE She did have kind of a silly look on her face while he was here. I just thought she was nauseous.

IDA Just you wait till one of you has a romantic caller. I'm gonna ridicule them just like you're doin' my heartthrob, my Dreamboat.

JUNE Heartthrob.

IDA I'm not ashamed of my feelings.

LETTY Dreamboat?

JUNE Nightmare you mean.

LETTY How long did you work for him, June?

JUNE I worked for his mother.

(Letty begins to read, half paying attention to the action. Ed enters carrying his sample case and Ernest's hat. Ernest is scurrying after him. They stop on the far side of the stage, away from the porch, to hold the following conversation.)

ERNEST   Ed, give my hat!   *(He grabs for it, but Ed holds it just out of reach.)*

ED   That's what you get for beatin' my time, Ernie, you asshole you.

ERNEST   You're not engaged to her as far as I know.

ED   Ernie, tell me. Did your pecker ever grow any after high school, or is it still that piddly little thing I remember from gym class?

ERNEST   Ed, yours wouldn't win any contests.

ED   Well, you little sonofabitch, you looked.   *(Holds hat in front of crotch.)*

ERNEST   You aren't captain of the baseball team anymore, you know.

ED   Let you in on a little secret. I'm still one helluva ballplayer. Ask Ida.   *(Winks.)*   Say, will you look at that. You stepped on a crack.

ERNEST   *(Appalled.)*   I just broke my mother's back.

ED   See you around, Ernest.   *(Plopping Ernest's hat on Ernest's head, Ed leaves him to stew and strolls up the walk to the porch.)*

ERNEST   *(Stands for a moment looking down aghast.)*   I'm sorry, Momma.   *(He exits.)*

JUNE   There goes his blood pressure again.

ED   Ladies, this beautiful day is now complete. My, it's good to be home.

IDA   What did you say to Ernest? He turned beet red.

ED   Oh, you know, this 'n that. I was talkin' a little math with him. Whether somethin' was two inches long or less.

JUNE   Less. I'd bet money on it.

IDA   You two are just awful.

LETTY   You know, Ed, talking dirty's a sign of middle age.

ED   It's a signa frustration because I never get the real thing.

IDA   Thank you for sharin' that detail with us, Ed.

ED   Ida, one of these days I'm gonna give up on you. I'm just gonna let Ernest Bogg sweep you off your feet. You'll be out to the Kentucky Fried eatin' a bucket of extra crispy while his wreckin' crew's turnin' this house into a parking lot.

IDA   Well, I'll be too in love to care.

JUNE   That'll be the day.

ED   Say ladies, do you know you are talkin' to the Midwest's Number One Salesman of Sheri's Lingerie for the third month runnin'? *(To Ida.)* I wish I could talk women outa their underwear as fast as I can talk 'em into it.

IDA   Ed, give it a rest.

ED   Ida, that's all it does is rest.

IDA   Ed!

LETTY   Yeah, Ed. I'm too young to hear this.

(Mary Ann appears in the doorway, rumpled from lying down in her clothes.)

JUNE   Look who's up.

IDA   You feelin' any better, Mary Ann?

MARY ANN   A little. Lying down helps. Oh hi, Ed.

ED   Hi there, kiddo. How's life treatin' ya?

MARY ANN   Oh, okay, I guess. But I am getting kind of worried about my brother. He's late coming home from work. Have any of you seen him?

JUNE   No sign of him yet, honey. He prob'ly just had a lotta dishes to wash.

IDA   Maybe he stopped off to the Rexall. Isn't Thursday when they usually get in a new shipment of comic books?

MARY ANN   Could you please tell him to come right up when he gets here? Thank you.   *(She exits.)*

ED   I never liked any of my brothers that much.

IDA   Well, I should hope not.   *(She exchanges a look with June.)*

ED   Guess I'll take this   *(His sample case.)*   up to my room before somebody trips over it. I'll be back down in a minute. You can talk about me while I'm gone.   *(He grins, exits.)*

IDA   God, what an ego.

ED   *(From offstage inside the house.)*   I heard that!

JUNE   Must be pretty thrillin' havin' both Ed and Ernest after you year after year, decade after decade.

IDA   Thrilling isn't the word.   *(Brief pause.)*   Boring is the word. I've known those two all my life, ever since grade school. Hell, Ernest and I were baptized together. Just once I'd like to date a man I haven't known since I was six. I prob'ly never will though.

JUNE   Well, you could do worse than Ed. I think.

IDA   Oh, honey, I have.

ED   *(Enters, one arm behind his back. He pulls his arm out to hand Ida a slim white box.)*   A token of my esteem.

IDA   If it's another one of your samples of crotchless underwear, I'm not gonna be amused.

ED   It's not a sample. It's not even underwear. Open it, Ida.

IDA   *(Opens it.)*   It's a two-for-one coupon for a ribeye dinner at Ponderosa.

ED   I'll even pay.

IDA   That's big of you, Ed.

ED   You name the night.

IDA   I better get my hair done first.

ED   I'll even pay for   *(Dramatic pause.)*   the dessert bar.

IDA   *(To Letty.)*   And you think all the romance is in books.

ED　　Say June, I saw your girl when I drove through town.

JUNE　　She comin' or goin'?

ED　　Don't know. She was just sorta standin' there. Just standin' at a corner waitin' for a light to change only it already changed an' she hadn't noticed.

LETTY　　I've done that.

IDA　　What time's it gettin' to be anyway? Ed, you got your watch on?

ED　　*(Checks his watch.)*　It's about a quarter after four.

IDA　　*(Standing.)*　Anybody in the mood to help me peel potatoes? *(No one speaks up.)*　Don't everybody volunteer at once.

JUNE　　*(Heaving herself stiffly to her feet.)*　I guess I've sat just about long enough. I'll give you a hand, sugar.

IDA　　Thank you, June. *(Narrows her eyes at Ed and Letty.)*　And thank You.

LETTY　　Hey, I made lemonade.

(June and Ida exit.)

ED　　*(After a moment passes and they're safely gone, he calls after them.)*　Ida, you sure you don't need any help?

LETTY　　Smooth, Ed.

ED　　Guess not. Guess I'm just gonna hafta go watch TV. It's a rough life.　*(He grins, exits.)*

(Letty takes her book and walks out into the yard, checks for a spot with no anthills or dogshit, then stretches out on the grass to read. The lights dim to indicate passage of a few minutes, then they rise again. Letty's head is down on her book. She's catnapping or daydreaming. Mary Ann is standing on the porch, looking like a fisherman's wife during a sudden storm. Ed enters loudly from house.)

ED　　*(Holding forth, aiming most of this at Mary Ann because she's handy.)*　You know what's on the four-thirty movie in there? I'll tell you what's on. *Death of a Salesman.* What a piece of crap. That is such a piece of crap I can't stand to watch another minute of it! That guy was no salesman. He was a loser from Day One. That show oughta be called "Death of a

Loser" not "Death of a Salesman." It's an insult to every good salesman who ever walked the face of this earth. And there've been plenty.

(Mary Ann has just been standing there.)

ED   I guess you're not into movies.

MARY ANN   We've got a TV set in our room. Maynard watches it all the time, so I do, too. There's no way not to.

ED   I like to watch TV myself, but Not That Garbage.   *(He says this last part loudly, as if the television set and possibly Arthur Miller can hear him.)*   All the good movies they could run they pick that one. Why don't they show *Maltese Falcon*? Huh? Why not?

MARY ANN   I don't know.

ED   Now that's a great movie.

MARY ANN   Maynard likes movies like *Rambo*, but I really like family stories. I used to love *The Waltons*.

ED   You from a close family, are you?

MARY ANN   *(After a brief pause.)*   No. I guess that's why I like watching. Those people are all so nice, and they all love each other so much. They'd do anything for each other.

ED   I don't know. That show never did much for me.

MARY ANN   You didn't like *The Waltons*?

ED   That guy with the splotch on his face got on my nerves.

MARY ANN   Really? Oh, I liked John-Boy a lot. He was my favorite. He really cared about his family. He was so sweet to his sisters. Letty, don't you wish you had a nice brother?

LETTY   *(Still reading.)*   Most girls that I know who have brothers wish they were only children.

ED   You from a big family, Mary Ann?

MARY ANN   *(After a brief pause.)*   Yes. I used to be.

ED   Are you from around here? You're not from around here, are you?

(Silence.)

ED   Guess that's none of my business.   *(To Letty who's reading.)*
You're gonna wear your eyes out.

LETTY   I don't think so, Ed.

ED   Whatcha readin'?

LETTY   *War and Peace.*

ED   That's by James Michener, right? You ever seen *Sayonara*?
Now there's another great movie. Wish they'd show that
insteada that goddamn *Death of a Salesman*. What a piece of
crap. You ever see that movie?

LETTY   No.

ED   That's good. You're not missin' nothin'.

(Silence.)

ED   Isn't ole Maynard home yet?

MARY ANN   No. I wish he'd come.

ED   He's gonna be late for supper if he don't watch it. I can
smell the meatloaf from here. Guess maybe I oughta go offer
to set the table. Show your mother what a swell guy I am.

LETTY   Mom already knows what a swell guy you are, Ed.

ED   Then why won't she marry me?

LETTY   Sorry, Ed. I guess she just doesn't want to.

ED   I've asked four women to marry me in my life and none of
them have ever said yes. What am I doin' wrong?! Even that
goddamn Ernest Bogg got a woman to marry him once. What
am I, a leper? I can sell anything. Anything. You name it, I
can sell it. I can sell a vacuum cleaner to people who don't
even have a carpet. Why can't I sell myself? Huh? Why?

LETTY   Maybe you're charging too much.

ED   I'm serious! I wanna know. If I asked you to marry me,
would you?

LETTY   No.

ED   Why not?

LETTY   You're just not—you're just nobody I'd ever be interested in. For a lot of reasons. Nothing personal, Ed. I don't think I'm ever going to marry anyone.

ED   Gotcha. Okay, so you're disqualified, but what about Ida? She likes a little male companionship. You're here to prove it.

LETTY   But I think I was sort of a surprise. Does that count?

ED   *(Mentally counting.)*   Your birthday's when? November, right?

LETTY   September. Mom and Dad got married in May. The same year.

ED   *(Still mentally calculating.)*   That is a little tight, isn't it? Well hell, that doesn't mean anything. I still say she musta liked him or you wouldn't be here.

LETTY   I don't see any more little me's around though, Ed. I've always kind of figured Mom learned her lesson.

ED   But I'd be such a great husband if only she'd give me a chance.

LETTY   Well then talk to Mom, Ed. You're talking to the wrong person. I can't help you. I'm sorry. This really is between you and Mom.

ED   I even asked a stripper once and she wouldn't even marry me. You'd think she woulda preferred a nice apartment with me over That wouldn'tcha? What do women want from me?

LETTY   Nothing, Ed. That's your problem.

ED   Well, I'm not givin' up. That's not my style. I'm gonna keep askin' her 'til she breaks down and says yes. I'm not the number one salesman of Sheri's Lingerie in the Midwest for nothin'.

MARY ANN   What time is it?

LETTY   About five, isn't it?

ED   Ten after. Almost suppertime. Guess I better go set that table. *(He exits.)*

MARY ANN   Why doesn't she marry him?

LETTY I guess she wants more—or less. I don't know. Why should she marry anybody?

MARY ANN He asked her.

LETTY She seems pretty happy the way she is. Happy enough anyway. I don't remember my dad, but I don't think he was very easy to live with. She's probably happier just sitting on the porch with June than she was married.

MARY ANN People are supposed to be married.

LETTY Even if it makes them miserable?

MARY ANN But it's not supposed to.

LETTY Do you know many married people who are happy?

MARY ANN *(After a pause.)* No. But they're supposed to be.

LETTY I think a lot of people get married who shouldn't, just to do what everybody else does. Then they're unhappy all their lives but they can go to church with a clear conscience.

MARY ANN I still think she ought to marry him.

LETTY Well, it's her life.

MARY ANN He's a nice guy. He works hard. I'd marry him if he asked me. But guys never want the girls who'll say yes. *(Self conscious.)* I think I'm gonna walk over to the Burger Hut and see if Maynard's workin' late. Would you please tell your mom not to hold supper for me?

LETTY I'll tell her.

MARY ANN Are you really gonna finish that whole book?

LETTY I've got all summer.

MARY ANN Bye. *(She exits down the street.)*

(Letty watches her walk away, then goes back to reading her book. Dinah enters.)

DINAH Hi.

LETTY *(Though still lying down, she jumps, startled.)* I didn't see you coming. Hi.

DINAH *(Drops to the grass near Letty.)* Where's Mary Ann going?

LETTY Maynard's late. She's walking over to the Burger Hut to see if he's working overtime. He could call.

DINAH Maynard's an asshole. Assholes don't call. *War and Peace?*

LETTY Ed thinks it's by Michener.

DINAH You mean it's not?

LETTY *(Shoves at her playfully.)* Smartass. I'll bet we're the only two people in this town who've read *War and Peace.*

DINAH And you've still got a thousand pages to go.

LETTY I'll finish it.

DINAH Where is everybody?

LETTY Getting supper ready. You must have taken a real long walk.

DINAH How was school?

LETTY Oh, you remember.

DINAH I loved college—still do—but I sure as hell hated high school.

LETTY It must have been really awful for you.

DINAH I don't think I ever exactly blended in.

LETTY Who does?

DINAH Well, being the only Black in an entire school system did make me feel pretty special. *(Brief pause. Then she slaps Letty's back.)* Mosquito. I missed. *(Her hand lingers.)* I like your blouse.

LETTY Well, you know me. I'm a regular fashion plate.

DINAH You Are pretty you know.

LETTY Right.

DINAH Well, I like the way you look, but what do I know?

LETTY I wonder if they need any help with supper.

DINAH   Smells like they're doing pretty well on their own.

LETTY   Maybe you ought to go tell June you're back. I think she was kind of worried, though she never says.

DINAH   No, she never does say.   *(Brief pause. Perhaps a glance around.)*   She sure is happy living here with your mom.

LETTY   Yeah, they enjoy each other a lot. They can spend hours out here talking.

DINAH   *(This observation is mostly to herself; at least, it starts out that way.)*   God it's silly. Such a waste.

LETTY   What?

DINAH   There are so many women alone in a town like this.

LETTY   So? What do you want them to do?

(Silence.)

LETTY   What?

DINAH   It just seems silly they don't . . .   *(She stops.)*   It just seems like such a waste for them to   *(Pause.)*   be alone at night. They sit on their porches together and they go to bingo. They talk for hours, share their most intimate thoughts, but they act like they can't go to bed with each other; they've got to wait for some man they don't like half as well.

(Silence.)

DINAH   Well, you asked.

LETTY   It's just that people here don't talk about it like that. Like it's okay. Like there's nothing wrong with being queer.

DINAH   I'm just talking about love.

LETTY   They don't call it that here.

DINAH   Well, the hell with them if they don't. It's still love.

LETTY   Nobody here wants to be queer.

DINAH   Lots of people want to be queer; they're just afraid to be.

LETTY   I should go set the table.

DINAH   Ed always sets the table.

LETTY   *(Blurts.)* Dinah, are you . . .   *(She stops.)*

DINAH   What? Hungry? Yes, as a matter of fact I am.

LETTY   You know that's not what I—oh, never mind.

DINAH   Am I what?

LETTY   *(Working up her courage.)*   Are you—Dinah, are you gay?

DINAH   Yes.

LETTY   Oh.

DINAH   Do you mind? Does it bother you?

LETTY   I've just never known . . .

DINAH   Oh, you probably have. You just didn't know they were. No one tells up here.

LETTY   Your mom doesn't . . .

DINAH   Know? No.

LETTY   How did you . . .

DINAH   Know? I met someone. I suppose I knew before, but I wouldn't admit it to myself. But then I fell in love and all I could think about was this woman and finally we—It was very convincing. I'm sorry. I'm making you nervous.

LETTY   I'm just not—I've just never really talked about it with anyone. Not like this. You really don't mind being gay, do you?

DINAH   Mind? *(Smiles.)*   No. I don't mind.

(Ida appears in screen.)

IDA   Time to eat. Come on, girls. Come in and wash up. *(She exits into house.)*

LETTY   No wonder it makes you crazy being up here.

DINAH   Well, there are some things I like.   *(Dinah and Letty really look at each other for a moment.)*   Like your mother's cooking.

LETTY   Asshole.

(They exit into the house.)

Scene 2

(A light change indicates the passing of the supper hour. June is sitting on the porch. Dinah enters.)

DINAH   How's your heartburn?

JUNE   Better.

DINAH   You need any Pepto-Bismol? I can go get you some.

JUNE   I'm fine. I took one of my pills. I know better than to eat French fries.

DINAH   But you still do it.

JUNE   Dinah, you may think you're perfect, but I know I'm not. Some days I eat what I'm not supposed to. It's not the end of the world.

DINAH   I just want you to take care of yourself. You're the only family I've got, so I don't want you dropping dead on me until you absolutely have to.

JUNE   Only family you're got! What about your brother? Doesn't he count?

DINAH   Not since he became a Jehovah's Witness.

JUNE   He's still your brother. He just doesn't celebrate birthdays.

DINAH   Mom, he lives in Texas. He's ten years older. He believes in Creation Theory. We have a hard time making conversation even the once a year when he calls to tell me they've had another baby.

JUNE   Leonard's still family. You've got family. You've got him and all of his kids and all sortsa cousins and aunts and uncles. And your father's still alive somewhere, miserable little nigger. What more family could you want?

DINAH Dad sent me a birthday card.

JUNE Isn't that big of him.

DINAH I didn't write back. It wouldn't seem right. You're the one who was always there, the one who raised me.

JUNE The man thought he had a career in tap dancing. Said he had to follow his dream. Tap dancing. God. People in the South out marchin' and dyin' for Civil Rights and that man was tryin' to get on the *Lawrence Welk Show.*

DINAH He runs a mobile home park in Arizona. He sent me a picture. *(She takes it out of her wallet.)*

JUNE Of him or the trailer park?

DINAH Both. *(She hands June the picture.)* He's playing shuffleboard.

JUNE Still shufflin'. Jesus.

DINAH I look a little like him.

JUNE You don't look one bit like him. You look like my mother.

DINAH You never told me that.

JUNE She just had a sweeter disposition.

DINAH *(Fondly.)* Oh, go to hell.

JUNE You helpin' Letty with the dishes?

DINAH Yes. *(Hesitates before exiting.)* Do you have a picture of her?

JUNE I don't need a picture of Mama as long as I've got you. All her hair fell out at a young age, but other than that you two could be twins.

DINAH Mo-om.

JUNE How's your hair?

DINAH My hair's fine. God. *(Shaking her head, she starts to exit into the house.)* Need anything?

JUNE Go wipe those dishes. I'm fine.

DINAH All right. *(She exits.)*

(June settles back to rock. Her eyes close. A moment passes; then Ernest Bogg appears, looking behind him as he walks, eyes darting about fearfully.)

ERNEST Ida? *(More of a howl.)* I-da! *(He turns to look up at the porch and sees June.)* June!

JUNE What you doin' back so soon? You were just here.

ERNEST Am I ever glad to see you.

JUNE That's a first. What're you doin' here? I thought you went home.

ERNEST I did. That's the problem.

(There's a brief pause. June doesn't say anything, figuring if she ignores him he might go away.)

ERNEST I was hoping . . . I was hoping you could talk some sense into my mother.

JUNE You know, Mr. Bogg, I'm gettin' old and maybe just a little bit senile, but I believe your mother's dead.

ERNEST But she's back.

(Ida appears in the screen door, enters.)

IDA Who's back?

JUNE His mother.

IDA She's "back"?

ERNEST Yes. She is. She's back.

IDA Ernest, your mother didn't just drive over to Mt. Pleasant to shop. She's dead. We buried her a year ago May.

JUNE I found her dead in her bed myself. Deader'n a mackerel.

ERNEST But She's Back.

IDA Let's back up a little here, Ernest. Just why do you think Elta's back?

ERNEST She is. I just know she is. When I got home, everything was topsy turvy. The furniture was tipped over. There was denture cream squirted all over . . .

IDA   Ernest, I never realized those weren't your own teeth.

ERNEST   Well, of course they are. *(He snaps his teeth together a few times.)* That was my mother's denture cream.

IDA   You held onto your mother's denture cream? Honey, now that's carryin' sentiment a little far.

ERNEST   It was in her room. Everything is. I left her room just like it was when she died. I couldn't bear to part with any of it.

JUNE   And now her denture cream's squirted all over?

ERNEST   *(Anguished.)* Yes!

IDA   So you think your mother's come back to haunt you?

ERNEST   Yes. Oh yes. She's back.

IDA   Ernest, you know if I walked in my house and saw my furniture all upset and I was tryin' to figure out who might've done it, I don't think my dead mother would be my prime candidate.

ERNEST   You didn't know my mother.

IDA   I did so know your mother. And I don't care how strong-willed she was, some things are just beyond anybody. Did you call the police?

ERNEST   What?

JUNE   Sweet Jesus.

IDA   Ernest, I think it's a whole lot more likely somebody's broke in your house than that your mother's come back from her grave. Let's go in the house and call the police.

ERNEST   You really think so?

IDA   Yes, I really do.

ERNEST   You think somebody's broken into my house?

IDA   *(Taking him by the arm.)* Come on, Ernest. Let's go inside and call the police.

ERNEST   Somebody's broken in my house!

JUNE   *(Mutters.)* My Jesus.

ERNEST   It was a burglar; it wasn't Mom at all.

IDA   I'd say there's a good chance of it.

(Ida and Ernest are at the screen door. She opens it.)

JUNE   You know, his mother did have a strong will. If anybody could come back, she could.

(A look of renewed terror passes over Ernest's face as he and Ida exit into the house. June waits 'til they're gone, then laughs. Dinah, Letty, and Ed enter from the house.)

JUNE   Dishes done?

DINAH   Yes, ma'am.

ED   What's that little asshole doin' back here?

JUNE   Somebody broke in his house.

ED   What's he doin' over here then?

LETTY   Oh, he always comes to Mom when he's got a problem. He always has ever since they were little.

JUNE   I don't know why she puts up with him.

DINAH   Who knows? Maybe she likes to mother him.

ED   It's not motherin' that little turd wants from Ida. I can tell you that.

LETTY   Ed, you take him too seriously. Mom doesn't take him that seriously.

ED   Now that's where you're wrong. Women like a man who needs them. Your mother knows I can get along without her. I'd rather get along With her, but I can get along without her. Now Ernest Bogg needs a woman to lead him around by his pecker. Women like that.

DINAH   Jesus, Ed.

LETTY   I don't want to lead anybody around by their pecker.

ED   Well, Most women do. It's a proven fact.

(Mary Ann enters from sidewalk.)

DINAH   Mary Ann, how about you? Do you want to lead a man around by his pecker?

JUNE   *(Chiding.)* Dinah. *(To Mary Ann.)* Honey, where you been? You missed your supper.

LETTY   Did you find Maynard?

MARY ANN   No. He left work at three.

JUNE   He's bound to turn up. Men are like that.

LETTY   Did you check at the Rexall?

MARY ANN   They hadn't seen him. They had some new Archies in, too. And a new Wonder Woman.

DINAH   Don't worry, Mary Ann. He's probably just off— *(She breaks off mid-sentence, because she can't think of anyplace reassuring he might be off to.)*

MARY ANN   Off where?

DINAH   I'm sorry. I don't know. I don't know where he could be.

MARY ANN   I don't know where he could be either.

JUNE   Mary Ann, haven't you ever heard a watched pot never boils? You just stop lookin' and' he'll turn up.

MARY ANN   Do you really think so?

JUNE   Hell, I don't know, honey, but give it a try.

(Ida enters.)

IDA   Oh, it's good to be out of that hot house. Isn't it a pretty evening.

ED   Where'd you leave that goddamn Ernest?

IDA   He's on the phone talkin' to the police. Somebody broke in his house.

JUNE   He was just convinced it was his mother come back to haunt him. I kinda like that idea myself.

MARY ANN   Somebody broke in his house?

IDA   It sure looks like it. But he wasted so much time callin' the police about it, whoever did it is prob'ly long gone.

ED   I hope whoever it was really soaked that little bastard. He can afford it.

JUNE   Not much there to steal. That's prob'ly why they made such a mess. They couldn't believe that's all there was. The TV's at least twenty years old.

IDA   I don't even like to think about someone breakin' into my house and pawin' through my things. I feel sorry for him. I hope he doesn't start havin' his palpitations.

ED   Palpitations. Jesus.

JUNE   You reap what you sow in this world, and that little pissant had some evil comin' to him.

IDA   Oh, Ernest isn't so bad.

JUNE   Try workin' for him.

LETTY Mary Ann, are you all right?

(Mary Ann just shrinks away shaking her head.)

ED   Hell, I'll bet ole Maynard just hitched a ride over to Mt. Pleasant to see a movie.

DINAH Mary Ann, would you like Letty and I to take a look around for him? I could use a walk after all that supper.

MARY ANN   No. Thank you, but you wouldn't find him.

LETTY We'd be glad to try, Mary Ann.

IDA   *(Elbows Ed.)* Ed.

ED   What? Oh. Oh, sure. Mary Ann, I'd be glad to check out the bars and stuff if you want me to.

MARY ANN   You wouldn't find him.   *(She moves further into herself.)*

DINAH *(Quietly.)* Maybe we better leave her alone. We tried.

LETTY *(To Dinah.)* God, some days I feel so alone, so lonely, but never like that.

IDA   *(Peering down the street.)* Look down there. That must be Midge Addison's new car.

JUNE   She said she had one on order. She musta just picked it up at the dealer's.

IDA   *(Peering.)* Why would anyone buy a white car? *(Squints.)* Or it that eggshell? Well, same difference. She's gonna have to wash it every other day or it's gonna look dirty.

JUNE   That'll be the day. That woman has a hard enough time keepin' her grass cut.

IDA   She says it's loaded. It's even got air conditioning.

ED   My old man used to drive around with his windows up just so people would think he had air conditioning. God that car would get hot.

JUNE   *(Rising.)* I'm gonna walk on down there and take a look while it's still clean. Wanna come along, Ida?

IDA   I better not. I should wait for Ernest.

ED   Jesus.

JUNE   How about you, Ed? She might turn on her air conditioning.

ED   Sure. What the hell. I'll go. *(He offers June his arm.)* Maybe I'll even offer to wash Midge's car for her. Get my hose out. You hear that, Ida?

IDA   I heard you, Ed, and you go right ahead with my blessing. You can even give her a grease job.

ED   I just might.

IDA   Well, go ahead.

(Ernest appears in the screen door, enters porch.)

ERNEST I'm sorry I took so long, but I was having palpitations so I had to lay down.

ED   So are you gonna go home now or what?

ERNEST But what if the burglar's still there?

ED   Aw, he's long gone. What d'ya think? He stopped to make himself a TV dinner while he was there?

ERNEST I think I'll just wait 'til the police call. If Ida doesn't mind. You can never be too safe.

ED   What makes you think this porch is safe?

IDA   Ed.

JUNE   Come on, Ed.

ED   You bet, June. I'm with you.

(Ed and June exit.)

DINAH   So the police are going to check your house?

ERNEST   They said they would. They said there've been several break-ins lately.

IDA   Is that so? It's a wonder we didn't hear that.

ERNEST   Well, it's been mostly cottages. Summer people.

MARY ANN   They haven't caught him yet?

IDA   Not that we've heard, but they prob'ly will. It's a small town.

DINAH   It's hard to get away with anything in this town.

MARY ANN   Oh, God.   *(She opens the screen door, is about to hurry into the house.)*

IDA   Honey, are you okay?

MARY ANN   I'm not feeling well. Excuse me.   *(She exits.)*

DINAH   Do you think one of us should follow her?

IDA   I don't know about you, but I like to throw up by myself. *(Lowers voice so Ernest won't hear.)*   It's that time of the month. Let's let her be for a few minutes.

LETTY   It's funny Maynard not coming home.

DINAH   Isn't it?

IDA   I sure hope it's a coincidence.

ERNEST   What? What's a coincidence?

IDA   Oh, nothing, Ernest. Girls, let's not start any rumors 'til we're sure.

LETTY   Poor Mary Ann.

IDA   I just hope she's not pregnant.

LETTY   Mo-om!

IDA   Well, it's possible. She hasn't been feelin' well.

DINAH   Who the hell would she get pregnant by?

IDA   Who do you think?

ERNEST   Who?

IDA   Never mind, Ernest.

DINAH   You mean they have sex together?

LETTY   Mary Ann and Maynard?

DINAH   Haven't you said anything to him? You haven't said anything to him! Jesus, you know it's gotta be him.

IDA   Dinah, what the hell could I say? I run a roominghouse, not a church.

DINAH   Somebody should say something.

IDA   Well, I don't know what. If you know what I could say to them and how to say it, tell me.

(Silence.)

IDA   Fine.

ERNEST   Ida, could you take my pulse?

IDA   *(Almost says no, but finally takes his wrist.)*   It's too bad there's been all this mess. This pretty evening is just going to waste.

LETTY   Smell the lilacs.

IDA   It's better than perfume.

ERNEST   *(Meaning his pulse.)*   How is it?

IDA   You're still alive, Ernest. You know, there used to be such a nice clove bush next door. Every spring I looked forward to the smell of clove. *(To Ernest.)*   I was mad at you for a month after you bulldozed through that clove bush. *(To the others.)*   He bought the house next door and leveled it just so he could extend his damn parking lot.

ERNEST   That's progress.

IDA   I wouldn't call it that. People drive up here to enjoy the beauty, our trees, fresh air. The Flowering Bushes. It does not make sense to bulldoze beauty just to put in more parking lot for your motel. Your customers don't come all the way up here from Detroit to look at more asphalt.

ERNEST   They've got to park somewhere.

IDA   At least the lilacs were on my side of the property line.

DINAH   You know, it Is a pretty night. All this—all this could fool you.

LETTY   What do you mean?

DINAH   It lulls you. Friends talking on a porch, smelling the lilacs—this town can seem like just the nicest place in the world to be. I almost forget what it was like being the town nigger. But I haven't forgotten.

IDA   Oh, I hate that word. Why do people use that word?

DINAH   Nigger's still what half the people in this town call me under their breath when they see me walking down the street. The really honest ones holler it out their car windows. Today I was waiting to cross the street, and three guys in a pickup drove by all redfaced—just seeing me standing there like I had every right to, insulted the shit out of them. They circled the block and came back when they thought of something to say.

LETTY   God. I'm sorry.

DINAH   Honey, it's not your fault.

LETTY   I live here.

DINAH   But you'd never do that to anybody. You're much too nice.

IDA   Dinah, you're gonna turn her head. Then you'll take off for East Lansing and we'll be stuck with her.

LETTY   I was walking home from school yesterday and this man—this wasn't a kid, this was a man—hollered, "thar she blows! Get the harpoon!" at me.

DINAH   Goddamn asshole.

IDA   Letty honey, you've gotta learn to ignore people like that.

ERNEST How can you ignore people who say things like that? Don't be silly, Ida. You can't.

IDA Well, what am I supposed to tell her? How am I supposed to help her? I don't like being helpless. I want to protect my child. You think I like listening to sonsabitches call her names? What am I supposed to do? Take a gun to them?

DINAH It's a thought. Might discourage them.

IDA I'll never understand why a person would deliberately choose to be mean.

ERNEST Some people are born mean. Others learn. Children are the worst. It's one reason I never wanted to have any. I remember what children are like. Nasty.

IDA They did used to say things to you when you were little, didn't they, Ernest? You were so little and skinny. But they didn't keep it up, did they? I don't remember anybody giving you a hard time in high school.

ERNEST It was Constant in high school. You just didn't see it, because you didn't see me. You were popular, and I wasn't. You barely spoke to me in the halls.

IDA Ernest, that is not true. Why I went to the junior prom with you.

ERNEST Only because your date got killed at the last minute and you'd already bought your dress.

LETTY Mo-om! Is that true?

IDA He's exaggerating.

ERNEST I am not. Her date, George Garland, was out drag racing the weekend before the prom. Rolled his car and broke his neck.

IDA I've dated some winners.

LETTY Thank God you didn't go to school with Charles Manson.

ERNEST *(To Letty.)* Your father looked a little bit like him. But then the army made him cut his hair.

IDA I just never had any sense about love.

DINAH Ida, who Does have sense when it comes to love?

IDA   Well, I finally did. I finally just stopped fallin' in love. I just stopped cold. And I started takin' in roomers instead.

DINAH   You can't just turn off emotion.

IDA   I did. Just like a light switch.

DINAH   I can't believe you wouldn't like to fall in love again.

IDA   Why should I? All it's ever caused me is pain. I'd just rather not reach out.

LETTY   Of course, she doesn't mean me. Right, Mom?

IDA   *(Hesitates just a split second.)*   Of course not, sweetie. I don't mean you.

(Hereabouts Mary Ann should appear dimly to audience, standing inside the house, inside the screen door, listening, unseen by the porch dwellers.)

ERNEST I wanted to go to the prom with Ida all along, but she was dating George, so I didn't dare ask. He was a real ruffian. Thought he was James Dean. He used to shove me into the urinals in gym class. Just give me a good shove in passing, just for the hell of it, just because he knew he could.

IDA   Well, George got his, may he rest in peace.

LETTY   Nobody asked me to the prom. I didn't want to go, but it's kind of depressing to not even be asked.

DINAH   You can bet nobody asked me. Every so often somebody'd offer to shove it in me out in their daddy's barn with the pigs, but they sure weren't going to be seen in public with me.

IDA   I'm glad your mother wasn't here to hear you say that. It would make her feel so bad.

DINAH   Well, I felt bad, too.

ERNEST Remember I bought you an orchid corsage? I knew you didn't want to go with me, but I wanted to pretend we were a great love affair. I used to be a great romantic before I got married.

(Mary Ann enters.)

IDA   Mary Ann, honey, welcome back. How you feelin'?

MARY ANN   Better.

IDA   Have a chair and join us. We're just takin' a little walk down memory lane.

LETTY   Bad memory lane.

DINAH   So far Ida and Ernest are the only ones who got to go to their prom.

MARY ANN   I didn't go to mine.

DINAH   Well, Letty and I are glad to hear it. Neither did we.

MARY ANN   I wanted to be asked, but nobody asked me. I really wanted to go. The girl always goes in the movies.

DINAH   Life isn't the movies, Mary Ann.

IDA   But every so often in a girl's life she wants to be a fairy princess, doesn't she, Mary Ann? I remember the day I got married I thought I was Audrey Hepburn. And I was. Or as close as I'm ever gonna get. I imagine the prom's the same thing.

MARY ANN   I felt really bad when I wasn't asked, but I wasn't surprised. I would've been surprised if somebody had asked me. I kept dreaming they would, though. I practiced saying yes.

IDA   It can be a painful time.

LETTY   *(Tongue planted firmly in her cheek.)*   What do you know? You got to go to your prom.

ERNEST   But she had to go with me.

IDA   Ernest!

DINAH   My god, he does have a sense of humor.

(Ernest titters at his own wit.)

MARY ANN   I didn't expect to get asked, because I never had new clothes and they said I smelled.

IDA   What a mean thing to say. You most certainly do not smell.

MARY ANN   Well, they said I did. Maybe I did. We didn't have hot water, so it was hard to wash. Maybe I did smell. The boys said I did. And the girls would never be my friend.

DINAH   You know, Mary Ann, some people've just got to have a nigger to feel better about themselves. It's not your fault you're the one they chose.

ERNEST   Of course it's not. People pick on me all the time and I'm clean as a whistle.

DINAH   Just get on with your life, Mary Ann.

DINAH   You don't know.   *(Mary Ann, as my mother would say, goes all inside herself.)*

(Knowing she needs privacy, the others turns their attention elsewhere.)

LETTY   Oh oh. Look down there. June and Ed are getting in that car. Midge must be taking them for a ride.

IDA   Will you look at that? She's even lettin' Ed drive. Brazen hussy.

MARY ANN   My family didn't have a car. My brother used to be so ashamed because we didn't have a car.

IDA   Isn't it sad how people make themselves miserable over things that don't really matter? Now my husband used to worry endlessly about his hair. He was so afraid he's be bald before he was thirty. Well, he was dead before he was thirty with quite a bit of hair still on his head. Wasted time.

MARY ANN   But things like that Do matter. Having a car. What kind of car. The clothes you wear. If your hairstyle's up-to-date. That's what they judge you on. That's what Maynard says, and that's how it was in high school. That's the last time I tried to make friends.

LETTY   She's got a point, Mom. People don't always get judged on whether they have a nice personality.

DINAH   And if you get called names long enough, something in you finally snaps. I remember a few years ago these two kids—little kids, I mean eight or nine years old—they hollered something ugly at me, something they'd heard from their parents. And I started to follow them. I didn't Do anything. I just followed them, maybe half a block back but obviously following them. After about four blocks of them looking over their shoulders at me, they started to run and I turned the corner and walked home. I just had to do something. I was out of control, and it was scary. I was scary. It scares me how easy that was, to decide to give those little assholes, those little kids, a scare. It opened up a side of me I'd rather not know is there. It made me realize I'd better spend my life someplace where I wouldn't be hurt like that day after day, driven to do shit like that or worse. I know if I'd stayed here, one day half the grade school would have been dead.

ERNEST I used to dream of bombing the lockerroom right before a game.

LETTY I don't want to kill them; I want to show them. I want to come back here rich and famous and show everybody.

MARY ANN I just wanted them to like me. Junior year, my high school held an assembly for people to talk about what bothered them at school. I stood up. I stood up in the gym in front of everybody, and I asked them why nobody liked me. I really wanted to know. I wanted to change. I wanted to do something, anything, so they'd like me. I asked them what was wrong with me.

IDA That took a lot of courage.

DINAH You shouldn't let other people decide what you should be, Mary Ann.

LETTY What did they say?

MARY ANN They wouldn't say anything. A few of them looked kind of embarrassed—they wouldn't look at me—but nobody said anything, so I sat down and the next kid got up. He wanted to complain about people spitting out their gum in the water fountain.

DINAH Poor Mary Ann.

MARY ANN I just wanted them to like me.

LETTY *(Cocks her head for a moment, listens, rises.)* Phone. Excuse me. *(She exits into the house.)*

ERNEST Maybe it's the police about my house. *(He starts to stand, then collapses back into his chair.)* My foot's dead. Oh my God, my foot is dead. The circulation's cut right off.

IDA Ernest, it's just asleep. Put a little weight on it. *(She stands and takes his arm, so he can lean on her.)*

DINAH I wonder if they caught him. *(She looks at Mary Ann.)*

IDA   *(With Ernest leaning on her.)*   There. Now put your heel down. Put your heel down, Ernest.

MARY ANN   It's all gonna come out.

DINAH   What's going to come out?

IDA   Ernest, you're not tryin'.

DINAH   Mary Ann, do you think it was Maynard?

MARY ANN   He promised.

IDA   *(To Ernest.)*   Aren't you feelin' anything yet?

ERNEST   It's tingling.

DINAH   It's not the end of the world.

MARY ANN   You don't know.

LETTY   *(Enters.)*   It's the police, Mary Ann. They arrested Maynard. He wants to talk to you.

MARY ANN   Do I have to?

DINAH   It's up to you. You should make up your own mind on this one.

ERNEST   Do you mean her brother broke into my house?

IDA   Shhhh.

ERNEST   He squirted Mom's denture cream all over my kitchen?!

IDA   Mary Ann, these things happen. This isn't your fault.

MARY ANN   Yes, it is. Yes, it is.   *(She exits into the house.)*

LETTY   The police said they found him in a house a couple streets over from Ernest's. The people are away on vacation, but a neighbor saw him break a window and called the police. Maynard had a gun and took a couple shots at them before they kicked in the back door and got ahold of him. Bail's going to be high.

IDA   She won't have the money.

ERNEST   Who wants him out on bail?

IDA   Ernest, stop leanin' on me. Your foot's awake now. Step on it. It's time for you to go home.

ERNEST   Alone?

LETTY   Mom, Mary Ann's going to need somebody to go to the police station with her.

IDA   That mean I'm elected? God. All I want is for everybody to be happy. Or at least act like they are. But everybody's just miserable. That's all anybody around here knows how to be, miserable. It just makes me so tired.   *(She exits into the house.)*

ERNEST   Ida! Ida, don't send me home!   *(Following her into the house.)*   I don't want to go home, Ida. Let me come with you. Please?

IDA   *(We hear her voice from inside the house.)*   Ernest, stop followin' me!

DINAH   She's right. She does have a way with men.

LETTY   Makes me kind of glad I never knew my father. I used to wish I had.

DINAH   I used to see mine now and again, mostly when he was out of work. Mom finally kicked him out for good when I was nine.

LETTY   Do you think you'd be different if you'd known your father better?

DINAH   Do you mean not gay? Hell, honey, I was born gay.

LETTY   That's not what I meant. I just meant—different.

DINAH   Well, I might be able to tapdance.

LETTY   Dinah! God, what a racist thing to say.

DINAH   The man tapdanced. I'm not kidding. Hell, he probably has rhythm, too, for all I know. I look a little like him, but Mom doesn't like to admit it.

LETTY   I wish my Mom would find somebody nice someday.

DINAH   Hey, she's got you.

(She and Letty look at each other. A moment passes.)

LETTY   And Ernest.

DINAH   And Ed.

LETTY   God.

Scene 3

(Half an hour or so has passed. Ida and Ernest have gone to the police station with Mary Ann. June, very recently arrived, is settling down to sit on the porch with Dinah and Letty.)

JUNE   Sounds like I really missed out. Musta been quite a show.

DINAH   It was a show all right. But it wasn't much fun to watch.

JUNE   I do feel sorry for that girl.

LETTY   Do you think Mom and Mary Ann'll get him out?

JUNE   They won't have the money. But at least this way Mary Ann'll figure they did what they could.

LETTY   Where's Ed anyway?

JUNE   Cigarettes. Midge dropped him off at the 7-11.

DINAH   I thought Ed was driving.

JUNE   Oh, he was for a block or two, but you know how Ed drives. Midge told him to stop strippin' her gears and he got mad.

DINAH   Well, that was kind of a personal remark.

JUNE   It feels good to sit.

DINAH   You only walked a block.

JUNE   I think I need new shoes.

DINAH   Did you take your eight o'clock pill?

JUNE   I'll get to it.

DINAH   Just don't forget.

JUNE   Dinah Simone, don't you treat me like I'm senile.

DINAH   Sorry.

JUNE *(After a pause.)* You still gotta go back day after tomorrow?

DINAH I teach summer quarter. That's when it starts.

JUNE You gonna be up for the 4th?

DINAH I don't know yet.

JUNE You'd think it was a thousand miles.

DINAH It feels like it's another world.

LETTY My counselor wants me to apply at State.

DINAH You should come visit. I'll give you the grand tour.

LETTY I don't know. Maybe. Thanks. I'll ask Mom.

JUNE I haven't been down to see you in years.

DINAH Well, don't brag about it.

JUNE You never invite me.

DINAH You know there's an open invitation.

JUNE That bus ride's hard on my legs.

DINAH So now it's a long hard bus ride. When it's my butt it's practically around the corner.

JUNE You've got a younger butt.

DINAH I wish you'd take your medicine. The suspense is killing me.

JUNE I wish you'd stop botherin' me about that medicine. I'd rather talk about Mary Ann and Maynard.

DINAH And I'd rather you took your medicine. You're half an hour late.

JUNE Well, I was an hour late this afternoon. It all evens out. Oh, hell. *(She heaves herself to her feet.)* You're gonna dog me all night 'til I take it, aren't you?

DINAH Yes.

JUNE I woulda taken it in my own good time, you know. I'm not senile.

DINAH   You said that.

(June takes a wild slap at her, intentionally just barely grazing her shoulder.)

JUNE   As long as I'm inside, I'm gonna go sit on the pot. Now I don't want you runnin' in there after five minutes just sure I've keeled over dead. I'm warnin' you now I'm gonna be in there for a spell, so leave me alone.

LETTY   Have a nice time.

(June points a finger at Letty, scowls, shakes her head, and exits. This leaves Letty and Dinah sitting alone on the porch.)

LETTY   What a night.

DINAH   And it's not over yet.

LETTY   I still can't believe Maynard and Mary Ann—you know.

DINAH   Most people do it with somebody. But God, to settle for Maynard. *(Dinah shudders.)* What a horrible way to learn about love. What a horrible excuse for love.

LETTY   I'd rather never be with anybody.

DINAH   Don't worry. You can do better than Maynard.

LETTY   Not so far.

DINAH   Mom's got her heart set on me marrying a white racist Jew just so she can suffer. Maybe I can find a nice white racist Jewish lesbian. What do you think?

LETTY   *(Laughing.)*   Yeah, I think that would go over big.

DINAH   Of course, it's not going to matter what she's like.

LETTY   It must be hard.

DINAH   That part yeah. But so much of the rest is really wonderful. It's the first community I've every really felt at home in.

LETTY   Sounds nice.

DINAH   It is. Music festivals lying in the sun with my shirt off surrounded by women and peace. It is nice.

LETTY I've never done that. Been naked outside.

DINAH You should try it.

(Ed enters loudly, breaking the moment.)

ED Hi there.

DINAH But maybe not here.

LETTY Hi, Ed.

ED *(Sitting between them.)* They got some new comics at the 7-11. Better tell Maynard.

DINAH Maynard's in jail.

ED You're shittin' me.

LETTY He broke into Ernest's house. And a bunch of other houses. Mary Ann and Mom and Ernest are down to the jail trying to bail him out.

ED Ida's off with that little weasel Ernest Bogg?

LETTY Ed, they're at the jail trying to post bail. They're not on the Love Boat.

ED I knew I shouldn'ta gone on that car ride. What the hell was I doin'? He'll be all over her.

DINAH Ernest?

LETTY Ed, you're nuts.

ED You just don't know lust, little girl. I do. I've known lust in my time.

DINAH Please don't tell us about it.

ED He'll be all over her like snot.

LETTY *(Just disgusted.)* Ed.

DINAH Just what is Mary Ann doing while all this is going on? Watching?

ED Hell, can you imagine that little mouse ever lifting a finger to stop a thing like that? *(Brief pause.)* Well, neither can I. I'm gonna go down to that police station myself and keep an eye on things. *(Exits.)*

DINAH   Jealousy is just an amazing thing.

LETTY   Can you picture Ernest all over Mom?

DINAH   I'd rather not.

LETTY   Ed really doesn't need to worry.

DINAH   Your mother never sleeps with anybody?

LETTY   Dinah!

DINAH   Well, honey, she is an adult, and your dad's been dead a long time.

LETTY   I'm sure she doesn't.

DINAH   There wouldn't be anything wrong with it if she did. Might be good for her. She seems kind of lonely.

LETTY   Mom? Lonely? She's always surrounded with people.

DINAH   Exactly.

LETTY   God, can you imagine Ernest naked?

DINAH   I've never been very interested in imagining men without their clothes on.

LETTY   Have you seen many girls naked? Jesus what a stupid thing to say. I'm sorry.

DINAH   Don't apologize. Yes, I have seen women naked. Have you?

LETTY   *(Pauses.)* In gym class. Mom. *(Brief pause.)* You the other night. *(She blushes.)*

DINAH   What? Where?

LETTY   I was outside looking at the stars. You forgot to pull your shade.

DINAH   Jesus, I wonder who else saw.

LETTY   Just me. *(Brief pause.)* And this tour bus that drove by.

DINAH   You asshole. You are kidding?

(Letty laughs. Dinah hits her playfully; her hand lingers. Ed appears.)

ED   Don't mind me. *(He hurries into the house.)*

DINAH *(Draws away.)* God.

LETTY What? Oh. You're afraid he might think—

DINAH I don't think Ed exactly thinks, but I don't want to do anything that might make life uncomfortable for you after I leave.

LETTY Don't worry about Ed.

DINAH It's me I'm worried about. And you. God you're pretty.

LETTY You really think so, don't you? You're not just saying it to make me feel good.

DINAH I'm saying it because it's the truth.

LETTY Dinah, I really like you.

DINAH I'm glad.

LETTY I like you better than any boy I know. But I—I'm just so afraid. Not just because you're a woman. I guess I'm like Mom kind of. I don't think I'm any good at this.

DINAH How can you know 'til you try?

(Enter Ed, rushing from the house with a lingerie box under his arm.)

ED Thought it might help ole Maynard if I brought a few samples for the boys down at the station. *(Winks.)* Something for their ladies. 'Course old Virg'll prob'ly wear one himself. That's guy's limper'n Ernest. *(Waits for a laugh that doesn't come.)* You girls don't have much sense of humor, do ya? *(He exits down the street.)*

DINAH I'm going to end up sharing a cell with ole Maynard if I don't get off this porch.

LETTY Why? It's not like we're doing anything.

DINAH No. But I want to.

LETTY *(After a brief pause.)* Oh.

DINAH Up here these assholes holler out car windows at you, and you're just so lovely. They can't see that, but I can. I can see the woman you're becoming despite them.

LETTY Dinah, I've never even kissed anybody.

DINAH   Well, it's time you did.

(Slowly, shyly, they come together in a kiss. Letty resists at first but then more than gives in. June enters from the house.)

JUNE   Well, I did my business.   *(She notices.)*   What're you two doin'?

DINAH   Nothing.

JUNE   Didn't look like nothing.

LETTY   We were just—

DINAH   Embracing.

JUNE   What do you mean embracing?

DINAH   We were holding each other.

JUNE   Did you kiss her? I thought I saw you kiss her. Did you kiss that girl on the mouth?

DINAH   Well, sort of.

JUNE   What the hell kind of answer is that? Don't you know what that might look like to somebody walkin' by? It'd look like you two were   *(A brief pause as she searches for a better word but can't find one.)*   kissing.

DINAH   We were.

JUNE   What?

DINAH   Please stop acting like you don't understand, Mom. You understand.

JUNE   You two were kissin' each other like boys and girls? That's what you were doin' right out here in the open, right out here in front of God and everybody?

DINAH   Yes. I'm sorry, Mom. This wasn't the way I wanted you to find out. I should have told you some other way. I should have told you.

JUNE   Dinah Simone, how could you do this to me?

DINAH   I wasn't doing anything to you, Mom. I was doing it to Letty.

JUNE   Have you lost your mind? She's a child. And she's a girl! All that talk in letters about women's bars and women's softball teams and never having a boyfriend and I never wanted to believe it, but you just had to rub my face in it. You're a goddamn bulldagger.

DINAH   Don't call me that.

JUNE   Kissin' little girls in the town where I have to live.

DINAH   Who says you have to live here?

JUNE   I moved here in the first place to take a job where I could finish raising you somewhere safe and pretty. And look at what I raised.

DINAH   I feel fine about what you raised.

JUNE   Well, I sure as hell don't. First you ruin your life; then you come up here to ruin mine.

DINAH   I'm not ruining anything. I was just trying to show somebody love.

JUNE   Show Me love why don't you! Why don't you?

DINAH   I Love You. And you know it.

JUNE   A freak. Some he-woman doesn't even know she's a woman. You live your life to torment me.

DINAH   Oh hell, I do not. I've got lots better things to do with my life.

JUNE   Like bugger white girls. Her mother is my best friend in the world! You should be ashamed.

DINAH   No, I shouldn't! I'm sorry you're too close-minded to accept me for what I am, but I'm not ashamed.

JUNE   You never accepted any decision I made in my life, includin' my movin' up here, so why should I accept every goddamn thing you do? *(There's truth in this.)*   Why should I?

DINAH   I just wish you would. I just wish you would.

JUNE   Well, I can't. I can't accept this. How did this happen? How could this happen? What did I do wrong? I must have done something wrong.

DINAH   Please don't.

JUNE   What did I do?

DINAH   You didn't do anything wrong, Mom. There's nothing
wrong.

JUNE   Yes, there is.

(Ernest, Ed, Ida, and Mary Ann enter from the street.)

IDA   *(Obviously exhausted.)*   Hi. We're finally home.   *(She goes to
her chair, sits.)*   We couldn't get him out. Bail's sky high.

ERNEST   *(Mutters.)*   Thank God.

IDA   Letty, while you're up, could you go get Mary Ann a chair?

(Letty pauses, glances at Dinah, exits into the house.)

DINAH   I'll help her.   *(She starts to follow Letty.)*

JUNE   She doesn't need your help.

ED   Guess I should go in pretty soon myself. Gotta sort my
sample case before bedtime. The B cups are all mixed up with
the D cups. Makes a worlda difference I can tell you.

(Uncomfortable silence.)

DINAH   How's Maynard?

ED   Mad he got caught.

ERNEST   He wrecked my house! And he could care less. All he
cared about was getting caught.

ED   He'll be out in a year or two, if that. Then he'll do it again.

ERNEST   They should lock him up and throw away the key.

IDA   *(To Ernest, looking at Mary Ann.)*   Shhhh. Ernest.

(Letty enters from the house with a chair.)

LETTY   Mary Ann.   *(She takes her arm, seats her.)*

IDA   *(To June.)*   She's in shock. Poor thing.

JUNE   Aren't we all?   *(She looks at Dinah, and Dinah looks back.)*

ED Ernest, isn't it about time you went home?

ERNEST Oh, I can't face that tonight. My pulse is just racing. God only knows what my blood pressure is.

ED If you're not goin' home, where are you spendin' the night? Your motel, I hope.

ERNEST Ida said I could sleep on the couch.

ED Ida!

ERNEST But just for tonight. She said I had to go home tomorrow.

IDA *(To Ed.)* And I told him you'd lend him some pajamas.

ED He couldn't begin to fill my pajamas.

LETTY Mary Ann? What are you going to do now?

MARY ANN What?

LETTY Are you going to stay in town?

MARY ANN I don't know where to go.

IDA Maynard's the one going to prison, not you. You just stay right here.

ED Hey, now you can even watch the TV shows you want to.

JUNE Girl, haven't you got any family? Other than Maynard?

DINAH *(With irony.)* You can always run to your family, Mary Ann. They'll understand. *(She looks at June, and June looks back.)*

MARY ANN I don't even know where they are. They don't want me anyway.

IDA Oh, now what'd you ever do to them?

MARY ANN Ida, you're gonna make me leave, aren't you?

IDA Now of course not. I said you're welcome to stay, honey. You'll always be welcome. It's not your fault Maynard turned out to be a thief. You didn't know.

MARY ANN *(After a pause.)* I did know. He did it before. I knew he did it before.

IDA   Oh honey.

MARY ANN   But he said he wouldn't do it again. He said he'd never do it again because of last time.

DINAH   What happened last time?

MARY ANN   He killed them.

JUNE   Who? Who'd that boy kill?

MARY ANN   A married couple. He was robbing their house and they came home, so he shot them. When they fell down, he stood over them and shot them each in the head—to finish them off, he said. Just like in the movies.

IDA   Oh God.

JUNE   My Jesus.

MARY ANN   He was fourteen and he ran to me for help. I knew it was wrong, but he was my brother and he was my friend. So I went with him. I'd never seen anything like that before. Daddy used to hang deer in the yard to quarter them, and I'd run and hide because alive they were so pretty. I couldn't stand the blood. But this was worse. These were people I knew lying there staring, lying there right next to each other all bloody. Maynard kept saying we had to get rid of the bodies and everything so nobody'd know. He kept pulling at my arm and telling me to help him, please help him. So I tried. We dropped all the bloody stuff in the river that ran behind their house. It wasn't very deep though, so the police found most of it hung up in the rocks. Everything was so bloody because we didn't know what to do about the bodies, so we tried to cut them up.

ERNEST   You Cut Up Their Bodies?

IDA   Take a nitro, Ernest.

MARY ANN   But then he found their car keys and he just had to go for a ride. That's how we got caught. The woman's sister saw us in that car and stopped by the house. I took some jewelry. That was all I took. I wanted to give it to the girls at school so they'd like me. But then we were arrested, and everybody knew what we'd done.

JUNE   Why did he do it? Why?

MARY ANN   He just had to have things like everybody else and
that was the only way he could get them. It was in all the
newspapers. Our mom and dad moved away with the other
kids before the hearings, and we've never heard from them. I
was put in the women's jail. Maynard was too young to try as
an adult, so they could only put him away 'til he was
nineteen. That's why he's out already. That's why he's out. He
promised me he wouldn't do it again.

JUNE   You were waitin' for him.

MARY ANN   I needed Somebody. And he was all I had.

LETTY   You just tried to be a good sister.

MARY ANN   That's all I tried to do. Momma wouldn't even come
see me, not once.

ED   Mary Ann, do you drink?

MARY ANN   No.

ED   Well, it's time you started. I got a bottle in my room that's
just the ticket.   *(He exits into the house.)*

MARY ANN   Ida, will you still let me stay?

IDA   Honey, I'm not only gonna let you stay, I'm gonna get
Ernest to give you a job as a motel maid.

ERNEST   Ida!

IDA   Ernest, shut up and act pleasant.

MARY ANN   I should've wondered how he could afford all them
comic books.

IDA   Live and learn.

ERNEST   *(To June, stage whisper.)*   She cut them up.

JUNE   Isn't that somethin'?

Scene 4

*(It's late. June is sitting outside under the porchlight, alone. Dinah enters
from the street; she's been walking. She stops when she sees her mother.)*

DINAH　You waiting up for me?

JUNE　No. I couldn't sleep. Sometimes rocking helps, but tonight I'm still wide awake and so are the mosquitos.

DINAH　Is Mary Ann asleep?

JUNE　I suppose. Ida was sitting by her bed talking with her last I looked. She's got her pretty well calmed down. She'll prob'ly sleep fine. 'Course the rest of us won't.

DINAH　*(Whispering loudly.)*　She cut up their bodies.

JUNE　It's worse than watchin' Alfred Hitchcock.

DINAH　Boy I'm sure glad I never went that far to be accepted when I went to high school.

JUNE　Hell, when did you Ever try to be accepted? You'd never even spend thirty dollars to process your damn hair.

DINAH　I think they still would have guessed that I'm Black.

JUNE　'Course now you're really showin' 'em you don't care what they think. You're really showin' all of us, aren't you?

DINAH　Mom, don't.

JUNE　You just break my heart.

DINAH　Mom, I'm sorry, but I'm too tired for this.

JUNE　You're too tired? I'm a lifetime of tired.

DINAH　You're going to start singing "Ole Man River" any minute aren't you?

JUNE　*(Rises.)*　I'm goin' in. I gotta get up early to clean the drugstore.

DINAH　I wish you didn't have to do that.

JUNE　I gotta make a living. There's always dirt to clean.

DINAH　When I finish my doctorate, I'll be able to send you money.

JUNE　I don't need money.　*(She looks at Dinah, exits into the house.)*

(A moment later Letty appears in the doorway. She emerges slowly, hesitantly.)

LETTY Hi.

DINAH Hi.

LETTY I hid out 'til she left.

DINAH I don't blame you.

LETTY Did you guys talk?

DINAH She hates me.

LETTY She doesn't hate you.

DINAH Well, she sure doesn't like me much.

LETTY Are you sorry?

DINAH Sorry she finally knows? *(Thinks.)* No. I've never felt comfortable hiding who I really am from her. This is something I've wanted her to know even if she's never at peace with it. Maybe that's mean, but God I'm not ashamed of being a lesbian. I shouldn't have to hide. No, I'm glad she knows. I just hope you're not too uncomfortable. After all, I get to leave.

LETTY I wish you didn't have to.

DINAH Really? It's a wonder you aren't buying my bus ticket.

LETTY *(After a pause.)* I liked it.

DINAH What?

LETTY The kiss.

DINAH Really? I'm glad. So did I.

LETTY Remember how I said I saw you?

DINAH Yes.

LETTY I stood there watching for a long time. I watched 'til the light went out.

DINAH That's okay. I'm just glad it was you.

LETTY A couple nights later I had a dream. You were in it.

DINAH What was I doing?

LETTY   You weren't. I was.

DINAH   What were you doing?

LETTY   Kissing you.

DINAH   Were you? That's really nice.

LETTY   Oh God I was kissing you all over. It was a crazy dream.

DINAH   No, it wasn't. I have dreams like that all the time. Some nights I can't wait to get to sleep.

LETTY   I woke up with my hand down there. I wasn't going to tell you. But I was afraid, after what June said—it's not like it was all you. I really wanted to kiss you, too. I was just so scared.

DINAH   Aren't we all? Everybody in this house anyway. You're doing all right.

LETTY   Am I?

DINAH   Absolutely.

LETTY   Can we do it again sometime?

DINAH   I'd like that.

(Ida appears in the screen door.)

IDA   You two comin' in soon?

LETTY   You need your shoulder rubbed?

IDA   *(Steps out onto the porch.)*   Did this bottle of Deep Heet give me away?

LETTY   Why don't you just have Ernest rub it for you?

IDA   Ernest is fast asleep on the couch. He fell asleep right after he said he'd never sleep a wink without his dehumidifier.

LETTY   I hope he doesn't take a liking to that couch.

IDA   He's been hinting around, asking how much I'd charge for the spare room Dinah's sleeping in.

LETTY   Mo-om! He's got a motel full of rooms just down the block.

IDA   But this is home. Sweetie, don't worry. I'm gonna send him packing in the morning. He and Mary Ann and I are gonna go over and clean up his house. We will if I can get a good night's sleep.   *(Hand rubbing her own shoulder.)*

LETTY   *(Hops up.)* Give me that bottle. Blackmailer.

IDA   *(To Dinah.)* Dinah, maybe you better latch the door when you come in. Jesus, it's gettin' to be a regular city around here.

LETTY   *(Holding the door for her mother)* After you, madam queen.

IDA   Goodnight, Dinah. *(To Letty.)* Thank you.   *(Exits into the house.)*

DINAH   Goodnight, Letty.

LETTY   Night. *(Smiles.)* What a night, huh?   *(She exits into the house.)*

(Lights down on Dinah alone on the porch.)

Scene 5

(Two more hours pass. Ida is sitting on the porch alone. Ed watches her through the screen door for a moment, then enters.)

ED   Hi there.

IDA   What's the matter, Ed? Can't you sleep?

ED   Remind me to buy a fan for my room before the hardware store sells out. I always wait 'til it's really hot, and then they sell out.

IDA   Tonight's hot enough. It takes the house half the night to cool off. I should plant some trees.

ED   Can't you sleep either?

IDA   I can't seem to get comfortable. My shoulder's kinda stiff.

ED   I could rub it for ya.

IDA   Thanks but Letty put some Deep Heet on it.

ED   You sure it's your shoulder keepin' you up?

IDA   Oh, it's lotsa things, but that's the easiest one to pin down.

ED   That was somethin' about Maynard, huh?

IDA   Poor Mary Ann. I remember when my husband was arrested for shoplifting. I was just mortified.

ED   Wasn't that why he joined up?

IDA   Uh huh. The judge gave him a choice. Jail or Vietnam. The idiot took Vietnam.

ED   You know, you haven't had the best luck with men, have ya, Ida?

IDA   Not exactly. Hell, if Maynard were a few years older, we'd be engaged by now.

ED   Don't joke.

IDA   "Don't joke"? Ed, are you feelin' all right?

(Ed shrugs. There is quiet.)

ED   What were you thinkin' about when I came out here?

IDA   Oh, you know. Things.

ED   Things?

IDA   It's kind of personal. It's   *(Brief pause.)*   hard to talk about.

ED   Oh.

(Brief lull.)

ED   Ida?

IDA   What?

ED   You bothered about Letty and Dinah?

IDA   What?

ED   Oh nothin'. I was just wonderin'. But if you aren't wonderin', then never mind.

IDA   What should I be wondering about?

ED   Well, they seem kinda tight these days.

IDA   I don't think they drink.

ED   Not tight like that. I mean *(Brief pause.)* they look at each other, you know, boyfriend/girlfriend-like. You know, like the way I look at you. I could be wrong. Maybe I shouldn'ta said anything. I just thought if it was botherin' you, you might need somebody to talk to about it, and I'm the closest thing to a man of the world you're gonna find in this town, especially at one in the morning.

IDA   You know, Ed, some days I just don't know why I put up with you. You can be such a blowhard, you can be so tiresome I want to put my hands over my ears and scream. But then times like tonight you actually say the right thing.

ED   You think Letty's gonna turn out to be a *(Brief pause as he searches for a diplomatic phrase.)* you-know-what?

IDA   I have wondered. I admit I have wondered. She follows Dinah around like a puppy, and she's always liked the girls best on TV. But I think I figure if I don't mention it it'll go away and she'll find herself some nice boy to marry. Not that I ever did.

ED   Marry me, Ida.

IDA   I was married once, Ed. It doesn't agree with me.

ED   Then at least let me rub your shoulder.

IDA   *(After a long pause, she takes his hand.)* All right, Ed. Come on upstairs.

(Ed, speechless, follows. They exit into the house. We hear their last two lines from inside the house.)

ED   You're not gonna let that little bastard Ernest move in, are ya?

IDA   Shut up, Ed.

CURTAIN

RAINCHECK

Cast of Characters

Grandma (Pansy)   a quintessential grandmother

Sister (Flora)   her senile sister

Thema   four times married, she's en route to her fourth divorce when she finds love with

Gwen   the county nurse

Setting

A living room in 1980s smalltown Michigan.

Summary

After four bad marriages, Thema moves home to live with her grandmother and great aunt, Pansy and Flora. When Gwen, the county nurse, comes to visit, Thema realizes what all her marriages were missing—a woman.

Author's Note

I like *Raincheck* for its sweetness and romance. I also like it because it goes against the stereotypes. In this play, it's the 'straight' woman who seduces the shy, hesitant lesbian.

Scene 1

(A cramped living room filled with knickknacks, a too-large sofa, a television, and a recliner chair with a phone right next to it. Grandma always sits in that recliner; she's sitting there now, reading a letter. We hear the backdoor/screendoor open and slam shut. A moment later, Gwen enters.)

GWEN   Hi there, Pansy.

GRANDMA   Well, Gwen. I thought you were about due.

GWEN   I just let myself in like always. How you been?

GRANDMA   Oh, I'm fine as ever. My urine still burns a little, but other than that I'm good as new.

GWEN   *(Taking her blood pressure kit out of a small case.)*   You do amaze me, honey.

GRANDMA   You always tell me I've got better blood pressure than a child.

GWEN   Better than me, that's for sure. And it's not like you haven't had your share of trouble.   *(Gwen is rolling up Grandma's sleeve.)*

GRANDMA   Did you hear about Thema and Rule?

GWEN   I heard they broke up.

GRANDMA   She left him.

GWEN   Yes, I heard that. About time is all I can say.   *(Attaching the blood pressure cuff to Grandma's arm.)*   I don't know how she put up with him as long as she did. She deserves better. *(Pumping.)*

GRANDMA   Rule's son emptied his rifle in her car door.

GWEN   I thought Ronald had to stay out of Michigan because of the warrants.

GRANDMA   I guess he got homesick.

GWEN   I guess.

GRANDMA   He and Rule got drunk as skunks and started breaking her dishes. Poor Thema. She'd worked so hard to put that set together. It took her months, buying one piece at a time over to the supermarket.

GWEN *(Reading Grandma's blood pressure.)* Good as ever. *(Pulling off the cuff.)* So's she gonna divorce him?

GRANDMA She says so. Maybe she'll change her mind after she cools off, but I really think this time she's had it with him. Of course, it'll be a while before she can raise the money for a divorce.

GWEN I'd be glad to pay her to divorce Rule. *(As soon as she says this, saying it makes her nervous.)* Wouldn't you?

GRANDMA She says after four divorces she ought to get a special rate.

GWEN God, there were four of them, weren't there?

GRANDMA This afternoon she's putting in her application at the hospital for aide work. And do you know she's even talking about wanting to drive a school bus? Can you imagine a woman wanting to do that?

GWEN Sure. Why not?

GRANDMA Oh, I'd be just petrified. I hated to even drive my husband's Ford. I just couldn't make left turns, so I only drove places where I could take right turns to get there.

GWEN Well, I know I've seen Thema left turn like a champ, so I wouldn't worry about her.

GRANDMA I do hope she finds something. Getting out and going to a job would do her a world of good. She says she doesn't mind being cooped up in here with Sister and me, but I'm afraid a few weeks of it might begin to make living with Rule look like a barrel of fun.

GWEN Oh, Pansy. *(Shakes her head.)* You're a card. So how is Flora?

GRANDMA She's on a counting streak right now. It's no real bother, but it can get a little tedious.

(We hear a door slam offstage.)

GWEN Flora?

GRANDMA *(Nods.)* She loves the bathroom. LOVES the bathroom.

(Grandma's sister, Flora—Grandma always called her Sister, and so will we—enters, counting.)

SISTER   29, 30, 31, 32, 33, 34 . . .

GWEN   Hello, Flora!

SISTER   Hello 35, 36, 37, 38, 39, 90!

GRANDMA   Have a chair, Sister. Rest your feet.

SISTER   *(Not sitting.)* They threw me out of that hotel, you know, so I've got to find some place else to spend the night.

GRANDMA   *(Speaking loudly to compensate for Sister's hearing loss.)* You've got a place to spend the night, Sister! Right here!

SISTER   All I want is a place to spend the night.

GWEN   Flora, you've got one. Right here!

SISTER   I said, "I'll give you nine dollars," but they said no dice, sister. *(She starts walking slowly toward the doorway.)* 9, 10, 11, 12 . . . *(She exits.)*

GWEN   Flora, your home is here.

GRANDMA   And she used to be such a good conversationalist.

GWEN   You must have nerves of steel.

GRANDMA   She wasn't always like that. It was all the fried food.

GWEN   Poor thing.

GRANDMA   Well, she gets by. Of course, I have to keep an eye on her, or she'll put butter in her coffee or wipe her nose on a candy wrapper. She's better some days than others. The weather has a lot to do with it. Overcast days you might as well be talking to the wall.

GWEN   Last time I was here she was in the bathroom looking for her geese. Do you know if she found them?

GRANDMA   Found what? Oh, her geese. No, I don't think she did, but she seems to have forgotten about them for now. She's more worried about where she'll spend the night. She keeps hunting for a hotel room. She knocks on all the doors in the house.

GWEN   She taking her thyroid pills all right?

GRANDMA   I slip one into her dessert.

GWEN   How about we take a look at your toe.

GRANDMA   Your life is just one exciting thing after another, isn't it, Gwen?

GWEN   And believe me your toe can't hold a candle to the colostomy I have to irrigate after I leave here.

GRANDMA   Thema's going to be sorry she missed you if you leave before she comes. But I know you're busy.

GWEN   Well, I would like to see her; see how she's doing. I've been wondering since I heard. How about if I dawdle? Let me go see how Flora's doing.   *(She smiles, exits.)*

(Pause, then the phone rings.)

GRANDMA   *(Picks it up.)*   Hello.   *(She listens.)*   No, Rule, Thema's not here.   *(Listens.)*   Rule, your boy shot her car door full of holes. She's got reason to be peeved.   *(Listens.)*   If I was you, I'd sober up a little before I said anything to her, Rule. You sound drunk to me.   *(She hangs up.)*

(Gwen re-enters.)

GWEN   Was that Thema?

GRANDMA   Rule. He's drunk.

GWEN   Isn't he always?

GRANDMA   Now my husband was a little weird, but that man takes the cake.

GWEN   Flora wouldn't let me in.

GRANDMA   She gets like that. Why don't you just let Thema take her pressure later. She's got one of those gadgets.

GWEN   Well, it's not really that urgent. It's usually pretty good. I just like to check it every so often. How's your toe feel?

GRANDMA   Oh, lots better since you took off the nail.

GWEN   Sometimes they get so ingrown it's the only way.

(The sock is off.)

GRANDMA There. I think it looks a little like hamburger, don't you? I call it my hamburger toe.

GWEN Well, it looks fine to me, Pansy. It's probably still a little tender, but it doesn't look a bit infected.

GRANDMA You do good work.

GWEN *(Laughs.)* Thank you, Pansy. I try.

(Gwen starts putting the sock and shoe back on.)

GRANDMA I just wish Thema would get back before you have to go.

GWEN Oh, well, there's always another time.

GRANDMA Remember how often you used to be over here when you and Thema were girls?

GWEN Yes. I remember.

GRANDMA You were such close friends way up into high school.

GWEN Then she got married. And I went off to nursing school.

GRANDMA Boys'll break up a good friendship every time.

GWEN *(Laughs.)* Won't they though?

GRANDMA Did you two fight over a boy?

GWEN Not exactly. *(She has Grandma's shoe back on, stands.)* I really should go. I should do Walt Cleaver's colostomy before it gets too close to suppertime.

GRANDMA Oh, Gwen!

GWEN I don't know what that man eats, but he has the worst colostomy in town. Believe me, I've seen them all.

GRANDMA Say, why don't you come back for supper? It won't be much, but I heard . . . *(She stops.)*

GWEN You heard . . .?

GRANDMA You haven't got anybody to go home to any more. I'm not trying to be nosy, Gwen. I swear.

GWEN   I know. You're a sweetheart, Pansy.   *(She leans down and kisses her cheek.)*   Tell Thema hi.

(The back door opens, slams shut.)

GRANDMA   I hope that's Thema coming in, not Sister going out.

(Thema enters.)

THEMA   Hi, Gram. It's just me.   *(She stops at the sight of Gwen.)* Well, hello.

GWEN   Hi, Thee.

THEMA   It's been a while.

GWEN   Seems like it.

THEMA   You look good.

GWEN   You look good yourself.

THEMA   Did you drop out of the Tuesday night league? Seems like an age since I've seen you.

GWEN   Didn't you hear about that?

THEMA   What?

GWEN   You must not've been there that night or you'd know, because it was a sight. I threw my arm back to throw, and I let go of the bowling ball. It sailed outa my hand and flew straight back and out the window.

THEMA   Oh my God, did it hit anybody?

GWEN   Lucky thing, no. I mean, being the bowling alley's upstairs, I coulda killed somebody with that damn ball. Broke in a million pieces when it hit the sidewalk.

THEMA   How did I ever miss out on that?

GWEN   I decided it was a sign that I should take up woodworking instead.

THEMA   It must've been a year or so ago when I had that awful flu. I was out for weeks.

GRANDMA   Gwen, you must have been just mortified.

GWEN   Well, it was hard to let on like that was what I'd planned to happen.

THEMA   I wondered why you stopped coming.

GWEN   Well, it's nice you noticed.

GRANDMA   *(Reels to her feet, grasping the chair to steady herself; she reels gently, as if aboard a ship)*   I hate to run out on you girls, but I've got to pee so bad I can taste it.

THEMA   You need a hand getting to the bathroom, honey?

GRANDMA   Oh, I can make it. I just have to make sure I start early enough. Especially if I have to stand outside the door and convince Sister I'm not the Mafia.

THEMA   We're gonna have to take the latch off that door.

GWEN   I wish I knew a cure for your dizziness.

GRANDMA   *(Reeling across the stage in the direction of the bathroom, holding on to furniture as she goes.)*   This inner ear trouble hasn't let up for thirty years; I don't imagine it ever will. I'm going to reel to my grave. And I don't mind just as long as the Lord doesn't think I'm drunk. I'll be back in a few minutes. *(She exits.)*

GWEN   She's amazing.

THEMA   Boy, she sure is.

GWEN   How'd it go at the hospital?

THEMA   Grandma told you?

GWEN   Well, I'd already heard the part about you and Rule. My brother works with Rule over to the machine shop.

THEMA   Oh, right. That's right.

GWEN   So I'd heard. It's just one of the thrills of living in a small town. Believe me, I know all about how little privacy a person gets in this town.

THEMA   I did get some hours at the hospital. Midnights, but beggars can't be choosers. So how've You been?

GWEN   Well, life's not exactly a motion picture, but I get by.

THEMA   I heard Betsy left.

GWEN   She just couldn't stand living here any more.

THEMA   I was surprised when I heard. Really surprised.

GWEN   It was just too isolated for her up here. That's what she said when she left. She was lonely. After a while just being with me wasn't enough. She wanted to be some place where she could blend in. Have gay friends. Pickings are pretty slim around here.

THEMA   There's that mechanic.

GWEN   Her and who else?

THEMA   *(Thinks.)* I guess I don't know.

GWEN   Actually, there are a few more, but I shouldn't mention names. They're still so far back in the closet the moths are after them. And none of them reads the books Betsy reads or knows music or art. She just felt stifled. That's what she said. And she got tired of little boys calling out things.

THEMA   You were together a long time. Probably longer than all my marriages put together.

GWEN   I still walk into the house and expect to see her.

THEMA   Where'd she go?

GWEN   New York City.

THEMA   Whew. I guess this town Was too small.

GWEN   She asked me to go with her, but I just couldn't. Of course, after she left I looked around and couldn't imagine why I wanted to stay here so bad I'd lose her to do it.

THEMA   Well, you're lived here all your life, except when you went away to nursing school. It's no wonder you wanted to stay. Who knows? Maybe she'll come back when she's had her fill.

GWEN   I wanted to grow old with her. She went to New York to feel young. She won't be back.

(We hear a stumbling step and counting. In the midst of the following numbers, Sister enters.)

SISTER   24, 25, 26, 27 . . . 27 . . . 27 . . .

GWEN   28!

SISTER   28!

THEMA   Hel-lo, Aunt Flora!

SISTER   They wanna do spikework in my house, but I won't let 'em.

GWEN   You stand your ground, Flora!

SISTER   I'll stand my ground if you'll stand yours.

GWEN   All right. That's a deal!

SISTER   1, 2, 3, 4.

THEMA   You were at 28 already, Aunt Flora! You'd made it to 28 already.

SISTER   5, 6, 7, 8, 9, 10 . . .   *(She exits, counting.)*

GWEN   You know, I'm awfully fond of her, but that must get so wearing.

THEMA   At least this time she thinks she's got a house. It's so sad when she thinks she's got to find a place to spend the night. I wonder if that bothers me because it's a little too close to home.

GWEN   Pansy said they were really busting things up.

THEMA   I've got great taste in men. God, I hope I've got the good sense not to do it again. Marry myself off to the first bozo who asks. Hell, they shouldn't even let somebody with my track record get a marriage license. I oughta be on some list like somebody who writes bad checks.

GWEN   You've probably said this every time. You'll change your mind when some man comes along.

THEMA   Thanks a lot.

GWEN   Well, honey, you did do it four times.

THEMA   Yeah, I know. I'm a little slow. It's taken me a long time, but I think I've finally figured out marriage is not somethin' I'm real good at. It's sure never made me happy.

GWEN   I'm sorry, Thee.

THEMA   Person gets tireda chasin' romance and never catchin' it.

GWEN   Well, take my word for it, catching it's got its drawbacks.

THEMA   There you go.

(Grandma reels slowly back in.)

GRANDMA   My, was that a relief. Thema, did you talk Gwen into coming back for supper?

THEMA   Honey, you didn't tell me I was supposed to.

GRANDMA   I told her it wouldn't be much, but we'd enjoy her company.

GWEN   Thanks a lot, Pansy. I appreciate it. But I've got some leftovers I should eat up. I can't break the habit of cooking for two, so I'm always eating leftovers.

THEMA   Aunt Flora eats with her mouth open, but if you can stand that, you're more than welcome to eat with us. I'm making salmon patties.

GWEN   That does sound good.

GRANDMA   You go check that old man's colostomy. Then hurry right back. We'd just love to have you.

GWEN   *(To Thema.)* You sure?

THEMA   I'd like it a lot if you'd come. We've spent too many years just sayin' hi to each other over to the Snowsnake Lanes.

GWEN   It took us five or six years for you to work your way up to hi.

THEMA   I know, Gwen. And I've been thinking, wishing for years we could patch things up. I just never quite knew how to suggest it.

GWEN   True. I couldn't really picture you and Rule and Betsy and me broilin' a chicken together. We stayed in the same town, but our paths really took a different turn.

THEMA   I know. And I remember when.

GWEN   Think we're adult enough to make up and share a meal together?

THEMA   Well, I'm game.

GWEN   I think I will come.

GRANDMA   That's what I like to hear.

GWEN   How about if I stop by my house and pick up my high school yearbook? We can look through it and laugh at our clothes.

THEMA   You always wore pants, even then.

GWEN   I wore black pedal pushers.

THEMA   With white anklets.

GWEN   I thought I was stunning.

THEMA   You were.

GWEN   But not like you.

THEMA   I did have the tallest hairdo in school.

GWEN   I'll bring that yearbook.

THEMA   I would get a kick out of seeing it. I lost mine a couple marriages ago.

GWEN   Do you need anything from the store? I'd be glad to pick something up.

THEMA   Not that I can think of. Gram, do we need anything from the store?

GRANDMA   Not that I know of, but I'll probably think of something the minute you're out the door.

GWEN   I'll be back in an hour, hour and a half, depending on Walt.

THEMA   I won't start frying 'til I see you coming up the walk.

GWEN   Thanks again for inviting me.

GRANDMA   We'll be seeing you, honey.

(Gwen exits.)

GRANDMA   You know, I've always liked her.

THEMA   Me, too.

Scene 2

(Sounds of cooking drift in from the kitchen offstage. Gwen is sitting, paging through an old yearbook. Grandma is reading the evening paper.)

GWEN   *(Calls out.)*   You sure you don't need any help, Thema?

THEMA   *(From offstage.)*   No, thanks. You rest your feet.

GRANDMA   Oh, dear. Will you look at that? The singing nun is dead.

GWEN   The who?

GRANDMA   You remember. The singing nun. She sang that song, that "Domineekeeneekeenee." They made a movie about her.

GWEN   Was Sally Field in that?

GRANDMA   No, she was the flying nun. This is a singing nun. *(Raises voice to call to kitchen.)*   Thema! Thema, who played the singing nun?

GWEN   Rosalind Russell? No, that was *The Trouble With Angels*.

GRANDMA   Did you ever see Loretta Young in *Come to the Stable*? Oh, that was a good one. The way I love all those nun movies it's just a miracle I'm not a Catholic.

GWEN   I still don't remember one about a singing nun.

GRANDMA   Thema'll remember. She's got a wonderful memory. *(Calls.)*   Thema, who played the singing nun?

(Thema sticks her head in the room.)

THEMA   The who?

GRANDMA   Who played the singing nun? I'm just sure there was a movie about her.

GWEN   Now we know it wasn't Rosalind Russell.

THEMA   I think it was Debbie Reynolds. Does that sound right, Grandma? Debbie Reynolds?

GRANDMA   Debbie Reynolds. You're absolutely right, but I never would've thought of her. Oh, I'm glad you remembered that. That would've bothered me all night. Debbie Reynolds.

THEMA Would you mind telling me what started all this?

GWEN The singing nun died.

THEMA You mean the real singing nun or Debbie Reynolds?

GWEN The real one.

GRANDMA Of course, she wasn't a nun anymore. It says here she left the convent years ago and had been living with a woman.

GWEN My, my.

GRANDMA She committed suicide. Oh, I hate to hear of anybody doing that. Especially if they could sing.

THEMA Dinner's just about ready. Gwen, would you mind rounding up Aunt Flora? I think she's upstairs talking to dead people.

GWEN Sure. Who knows? Maybe it's somebody I know. Let's just hope they weren't my patients. *(She exits.)*

GRANDMA She's such a sweet girl. I'm surprised you ever stopped being friends with her, Thema. I never understood that.

THEMA I had my reasons. They seem pretty stupid now, but I did have my reasons.

GRANDMA She's kind. Not many people are any more. I treasure kindness in a person.

THEMA It is rare.

(In the course of the conversation, Grandma has risen from her chair; Thema offers her her arm to walk her to the kitchen.)

GRANDMA I'll bet you two are going to be great friends again. I'll just bet you will.

THEMA I wish that were true, Gram, but I kinda doubt Gwen wants to be my friend. I let her down pretty hard when we were teenagers.

GRANDMA I think she'd let that be water under the bridge if you would, honey.

THEMA Well, we'll see.

(They exit.)

(There is a light change to indicate the passing of an hour or so. Thema and Gwen enter the living room from the kitchen.)

THEMA   Thanks for wiping.

GWEN   Thank you for supper.

THEMA   *(Notices that the yearbook is open.)*   You started without me.

GWEN   That's all right. I can look at these old pictures for hours. We can turn back to the beginning.

(Thema picks up the yearbook, sits on the couch. Gwen hesitates, then sits on the couch next to her. Thema opens the yearbook.)

THEMA   I'd like that. Will you look at all the things people wrote in here. Did I write something?

GWEN   I suppose. I don't really remember.   *(She gestures with her head toward the kitchen.)*   You know it's amazing Flora can still play cards like that as bad as her mind is.

THEMA   *(Eyes down, reading the yearbook.)*   She's always loved to play cards; some part of her remembers. She's not very good, but it is amazing she can play at all. Grandma makes a point of seeing they play every night after supper. She figures it's good for Aunt Flora's mind. She says it "stimulates" her. *(Referring to the yearbook.)*   My, I had no idea you and Cindy Baylor were so close. And to think she's the mother of five.

GWEN   *(Blushes.)*   She was just a friend.

THEMA   Right.

GWEN   I was kind of surprised when she got married, but I guess that's what everybody did back then.

THEMA   Everybody but you.

GWEN   Thank God. Or "the Goddess" as Betsy would say.

THEMA   You knew yourself better than most. What's this blotch here.

GWEN   *(Embarrassed.)*   Some guy got his hands on it and wrote "lesbo." I poured half a bottle of ink on it.

THEMA   What a rotten thing to do. Do you remember who it was?

GWEN   I believe it was your first husband.

THEMA   That asshole.

GWEN   Doesn't matter. That's a long time ago.

THEMA   I never said anything to him, Gwen.

GWEN   Let's look at the pictures.

THEMA   Did you meet Betsy in nursing school?

GWEN   Nope. Will you look at you in this picture? God, I wish it was in color. Look at your lipstick.

THEMA   Oh, I looked awful. It's a wonder anybody asked me out. Turn the page.

GWEN   You were one of the prettiest girls in school, and you know it. Everybody looked like that.

THEMA   Not you.

GWEN   Let's just say we both prefer the way we look now.

THEMA   You don't like to talk about Betsy, do you?

GWEN   Do you like to talk about Rule? Oh, God. Those two don't belong in the same breath.

THEMA   Are you insulting my husband?

GWEN   *(After the moment it takes her to realize Thema's kidding.)* I hear his son shot up your car.

THEMA   Ronald's real fond of me.

GWEN   You should call the police.

THEMA   Wouldn't do a bit of good. It'd just make them mad. Rule'd bail him out. Then they'd come over here and shoot up the other side of my car. No thanks. I just want to be left in peace to hide out here with Grandma and Aunt Flora 'til I'm old and gray.

GWEN   That'd be an awful waste, Thema.

THEMA   Well, isn't that what you're doing? Living alone but cooking for two, keeping your memory of Betsy all locked up inside yourself?

(Pause.)

GWEN   Let's look at the pictures.

THEMA   Rule couldn't hurt me the way Betsy hurt you, because I
was so long past loving him. I don't know as I ever really did
love him. How can you love a man who keeps his socks up
with the rings off canning jar lids?

GWEN   *(Laughing.)*   Oh, God, Thee, does he?

THEMA   Oh, and worse. But I wanted a roof over my head, so I put
up with it. 'Til now. 'Til I finally—Finally reached my limit.

GWEN   I'm glad.

THEMA   Are you?

GWEN   For your sake.

THEMA   Just for my sake?

GWEN   I'm just glad.

THEMA   You always said you wanted what was best for me.

GWEN   But we sure disagreed about what that was, didn't we?

THEMA   I was afraid. You weren't. God, you had a lot of guts.

GWEN   Honey, it wasn't guts. I just didn't know any better. And
I'm so bullheaded it sure took me a long time to learn. I didn't
learn my lesson from what happened with you. Cindy Baylor's
brother beat me half to death when he read a letter I sent
her. Hell, that didn't even do it. I brought Betsy here to live
like I had every right to; didn't think a thing of it. My parents
wouldn't talk to me for a year. Now That made me think
twice. If my own parents could turn on me, think what
Everybody else might do. So we were cautious. So cautious it
finally drove her away.

THEMA   My mom was a sweet woman, but she was afraid of
everything. Mice. Storms. What people thought. It rubbed off
on me early. She was so scared of airplanes. The one time she
gave in and took a plane with my father—

GWEN   It crashed.

THEMA   That did give me pause.

GWEN   I guess that would sorta back up her point of view.

THEMA   But I'm beginning to think maybe I've spent my life being afraid of the wrong things.

(Sister wanders in from the kitchen.)

GWEN   I've enjoyed talking. I don't get much chance to.

THEMA   Any time.

GWEN   Well, we'll see.

THEMA   The game must be over.

SISTER   I have to get home. I'm expecting company, and I have to get home to cook the meal. I'm almost too late as it is. I don't know if the roast'll get done or not. Well, if it's not done, they'll just have to eat it bloody.

THEMA   Aunt Flora, we already had supper! Don't you remember? We had salmon patties! You ate two of them.

SISTER   No one will ever take me home. I ask and I ask and no one will take me.

THEMA   How about if I take you up to your room, to your home—how about that? *(Lacing her aunt's arm through her own.)* Would you like me to take you home, Aunt Flora?

SISTER   Do you know the way?

THEMA   Yes, Aunt Flora, you just lean on me. *(In a quieter voice to Gwen.)* I'll be right back.

GWEN   I should get going. I really should.

THEMA   *(Walking with Sister.)* Wait. Please? I'll be right back. Just let me tuck her in.

SISTER   1, 2, 3, 4.

THEMA   5, 6, 7, 8.

SISTER   9.

THEMA   10.   *(Under her breath.)* I'll be right back.

(Thema and Sister exit. Gwen picks up the yearbook. She looks at a picture.)

GWEN You weren't one of the prettiest girls in school. You were The prettiest. *(Her finger traces the picture.)*

(Grandma enters. Gwen is startled, closes the book.)

GRANDMA Did Sister pass this way?

GWEN Thema took her up to her room.

GRANDMA Oh, good. That's a relief. It's so nice having Thema here to help.

GWEN I imagine it must be.

GRANDMA But, you know, I worry about that girl. She needs to get out more.

GWEN She will. It just may take her a little while. Healing takes a while.

GRANDMA *(Joking.)* Well, you're the nurse, Gwen. Can't you heal her?

GWEN *(Flabbergasted but tries to hide it.)* I don't know, Pansy. I'm really better at taking off toenails than I am at healing broken hearts.

(Grandma is, by now, sitting in her chair.)

GRANDMA Thema's still awfully fond of you. I can tell. I wish you two would get to be friends again. It would be good for the both of you.

GWEN Well, we'll see. *(She checks her watch.)* You know, it's getting late. I really should get going. I have to let my dog out. Get to bed. You know. Tell Thema bye for me, will you? And thank her again for supper. How about next week I bring over a bucket of chicken to pay you back?

GRANDMA You don't have to pay us back, honey. We love having you here.

GWEN *(Smiles, suddenly shy.)* I like being here. You have a nice evening, Pansy. What's left of it. Night. *(She exits.)*

GRANDMA Goodnight, Gwen.

(A pause, then Thema enters.)

THEMA Gwen? Oh, hi, Grandma. Where's Gwen?

GRANDMA Gwen had to go home and let her dog out. She said to tell you bye and thank you for supper.

THEMA I wish she'd stayed. We'd hardly even started looking at her yearbook. *(She notices it on the couch.)* Oh, she left it. I wonder if she meant to.

GRANDMA You two still make each other uncomfortable, don't you?

THEMA A little, I guess.

GRANDMA You should try and get over it. A person doesn't make that many true friends in this life. Sister was my best friend for as long as I can remember. Now that her mind's off in orbit, I miss having her to talk to.

THEMA *(Sitting, yearbook in her hands.)* You can talk to me, Grandma.

GRANDMA Oh, and I do. About some things. But other times a person just needs somebody their own age. Somebody who remembers the same things you do. Sister and I shared so much of our lives. We have so many memories in common, and now I'm the only one who remembers them.

THEMA I think Gwen and I remember too much.

GRANDMA Sister and I are the last of seven children. She's the only person left in the world who grew up out on that homestead farm with me. She stood up with me at my wedding. She stood by me after your parents died in that plane accident. She and I've been through it all together. I just wish she remembered.

THEMA Gram, I'm more than willing to spend time with Gwen. I'd like to get to know her again. But I'm not a bit sure she wants to spend time with me. Look at tonight. She practically ran out of the house.

GRANDMA She said she'd come by next week with a bucket of chicken. That doesn't sound like someone who's running to me.

THEMA I just wish she'd stayed tonight.

GRANDMA Oh, you'd complain if they hung you with a new rope.

THEMA   Probably. Here's a picture of her in her band uniform. She was so striking. She wasn't pretty, she wasn't soft, she was striking. She still is.

GRANDMA   Yes, she is. She certainly is.

THEMA   Look at this. I did write something in here. "Good luck in your nursing career. Sincerely, Thema." My, that's warm. Jesus, it's a wonder she talks to me at all.

GRANDMA   Don't wait 'til one of you goes senile to make friends with her again, honey. Time doesn't last forever.

THEMA   Can I embroider that on a pillow, Grandma?

GRANDMA   Turn on the television.

Scene 3

(Grandma is sitting reading Guideposts. *Sister is sitting fishing in her bra. The screen door opens and closes offstage. Gwen enters.)*

GWEN   Hi there.

GRANDMA   *(Just a little startled. She hadn't heard the door.)*   Well, hello, Gwen. You know I can't get used to that door since Thema fixed the spring. It's so quiet.

SISTER   I lost everything in the Depression, even my teeth.

GRANDMA   It must be going to rain. Sister's mind is really in orbit today.

GWEN   What's she looking for down there anyway? Her teeth?

SISTER   I lost Everything in the Depression. Even my Teeth.

GRANDMA   I think her glasses may be in her brassiere, but I'm too shy to look.

GWEN   Want me to?

GRANDMA   Oh, no, no. Let her fish. It gives her something to pass the time.

SISTER   I had to gum everything I ate.

GWEN   I'm just on my way over to the cemetery. I cut several buckets of lilacs. I'm gonna put one on my parents' grave. I

was wondering if you'd like me to put some on any of your
family graves.

GRANDMA Aren't you sweet. You know, Thema's mother just loved
lilacs. Just loved them. Now I don't think my husband would
get much out of them—he had no sense of smell—but I think
Genevieve would really appreciate some.

GWEN How about you, Flora? Do you think your husband would
appreciate some flowers on his grave?

SISTER He's out in the yard. *(Rising.)* I'll go ask him. *(She is
exiting.)*

GWEN No, Flora, wait!

SISTER He shouldn't be working out in the sun like that anyway.
You wait. I'll go ask him. *(She exits.)*

GWEN But Flora, you can't ask him! He's dead!

GRANDMA Who knows? Maybe she'll get an answer. I wouldn't put
it past her.

(Thema enters.)

THEMA Grandma— *(She see Gwen.)* Oh. Gwen. Hi. Gram,
Mr. Lindberg's out on the porch. He wants to read your palm.
(To Gwen.) He says she's got the longest lifeline in town.

GWEN I wouldn't be a bit surprised. Who's Mr. Lindberg?

THEMA Oh, he's one of Grandma's many flames. He's a widower.
Lives down the street in the old Wilson house.

GWEN Well, he must be in pretty good shape if I've never met him.

GRANDMA *(Has reeled to her feet.)* He's only seventy-one, so he's
way too young for me, but now if he were ten years older I
might take him seriously. Tell Thema about the lilacs. Oh,
and if Flora's gone too long you'd better go hunt her up. I
don't think she's going to find Axel out in the yard. *(She exits.)*

THEMA What was that all about?

GWEN I've got some buckets of lilacs in my car. I cut a whole
bunch of them to take over to the cemetery. Today's my
mother's birthday, and I wanted to take her flowers. I stopped
by to see if Pansy or Flora or you would like me to put any on
your family graves.

THEMA   That's really nice, Gwen.

GWEN   Well, I've got tons. They smelled so pretty I kinda went wild.

THEMA   You really are very sweet. Who else do I know who would do something like this on their mother's birthday?

GWEN   Pansy said your mother would like some. And Flora's out in the yard asking Axel if he'd like a bucket on his grave.

THEMA   What's he doing out in the yard?

GWEN   I don't know, but whatever it is he's doing it in the sun, and she's afraid he's going to die of sunstroke.

THEMA   He did.

GWEN   See? She's got good cause to worry.

THEMA   Gwen, would you mind if I rode along? I've been wanting to visit my parents' grave; trim the grass away from the stone.

GWEN   I put the grass clippers in the car. Why don't you come? That way you can pick out which lilacs your mother would like. There's several shades.

THEMA   Just let me change my shoes.

GWEN   Go ahead. I'll tell Pansy we're going.

THEMA   Just don't sneak up on them.

GWEN   If you'd stop fixing everything I could slam a few doors.

THEMA   I'm proud of those doors. I never fixed one before, never in my whole life, but I finally just took a book out of the library. I always thought I had to beg Rule, and hell there wasn't anything to it.

GWEN   You can do anything you put your mind to, Thee.

THEMA   I'm almost starting to believe that.

GWEN   After we get done at the cemetery, will you let me buy you supper? I just love that salad bar out to the Bonanza.

THEMA   Well, I don't know, I . . .

GWEN *(Interrupts.)* That's all right. You don't need to explain.

THEMA No, it's not that.

GWEN Not what?

THEMA What you were thinking.

GWEN What was I thinking?

THEMA That I'm afraid of you.

GWEN Well, maybe you're just afraid to be seen with me. I can understand that. People might talk.

THEMA Gwen, I defrosted some meat to cook Grandma and Aunt Flora a meatloaf for supper. That's all I was thinking of when I hesitated. Boy, I sure burned you bad, didn't I?

GWEN Yes, but you'd think I'd forget about it, wouldn't you? After all these years?

THEMA I wish you would.

GWEN How about if I treat everybody to the Bonanza?

THEMA How about if you come back here for meatloaf? We never did finish looking at that yearbook. It's still here, you know. I'd really like to look at it with you.

(Pause.)

GWEN All right.

THEMA I won't bite, Gwen.

GWEN Change your shoes.

Scene 4

(Grandma and Sister are sitting in the living room.)

GRANDMA Isn't it nice having someone do all the cooking and wash the dishes? We're going to get spoiled, Sister.

(No reply; Sister's staring into space.)

GRANDMA *(Referring to Sister's glassy stare.)* All the lights are on, but nobody's home. Ah well, I guess it's a break from the counting. Are you listening, Sister? I'm glad to see Thema and Gwen getting friendly again, aren't you? They like each other; you can tell they do. They're just a little skittish. They don't know who they can trust. But people have to have friends. And they were such close friends in high school. Do you remember that, Sister? They preferred each other's company over everyone else. The boys would come panting after them like puppies, but they'd just turn up their noses. Of course then, all of a sudden, Thema was dating any boy who'd ask, and Gwen couldn't even get her to talk to her on the phone. I never knew exactly why they stopped being friends. I guess I just figured that's what happens to friendships, even the best friendships, when boys enter the picture.

SISTER We ate lard sandwiches and slept where we could in the Depression.

GRANDMA Yes, Sister, I remember. You and Axel had a hard time of it in the city. I was glad when you moved back here.

(Gwen and Thema enter in time to hear Sister's next line.)

SISTER I ate a rat once. Boiled it.

THEMA Did my meatloaf remind you of boiled rat, Aunt Flora?

GRANDMA Your meatloaf was delicious, Thema. Sister's just recalling the Depression.

SISTER Did you ever gut a rat?

GWEN I don't believe so. How about you, Thee?

THEMA Not that I remember.

SISTER Big rat. I had to kill him with a shovel.

GRANDMA It's so sad when she talks like this. I wonder and wonder if it's the truth. She did have some hard years in the Thirties, but she'd never talk about her troubles when she was going through them.

SISTER Axel cried that night to think we were so low we had to eat rat. I don't think he ever quite got over it.

GRANDMA I'll just bet it's all true.

GWEN You work tonight, Thema?

THEMA Yes, I do.

GWEN Would you like me to go, so you can sleep for a little bit?

THEMA No. I'd rather you didn't go.

SISTER I split it right down its belly and gutted it.

GRANDMA Sister, I think it's about time for our card game. The kitchen table's clear. *(Rising.)* Come along with me, honey. You need a change of subject, especially so soon after we've all eaten. *(Nearing Sister, she grasps her arm.)* Here, let me lean on you. We'll see you later, girls.

SISTER We boiled it and boiled it.

GRANDMA I'm sure you did, Sister.

(Grandma and Sister exit, Grandma leaning on Sister for her balance, Sister straight and steady, shuffling along beside her.)

THEMA I don't know what I'll do when she dies.

GWEN I used to feel that way about Betsy. I always thought we'd grow old together.

THEMA Where did you meet her?

GWEN In a bar.

THEMA Where?

GWEN A women's bar—a lesbian bar—in Chicago. We talked. I bought her a drink. She bought me one. We danced. A week later, she came back here with me to live.

THEMA Wow, you must really be something.

GWEN I guess she thought so. For a while.

THEMA The first time I saw you together I thought, she's finally found what she wanted. That woman's just crazy about her. The way Betsy looked at you, she just laid herself bare.

GWEN She wasn't used to small towns. It took her a while to learn to be careful; to wait 'til we got home. She never did like it. She never got used to it. *(Pause, then she mentally shakes herself.)* Do you want to look at the yearbook?

THEMA   The yearbook? Oh, the yearbook. I guess. Is that what you want to do?

GWEN   Well, if you don't want to—I know it's getting late . . .

THEMA   Don't run away.

GWEN   Thee, I know you want to be friends again, but I don't know if I can.

THEMA   Oh.

GWEN   Honey, it's not because I'm mad about what happened. That was a long time ago. And it's not that I don't like you. I do like you. That's the problem.

THEMA   Why is that a problem?

GWEN   Oh, come on, Thema. You were pretty naive in high school—we both were. You're not naive anymore. You know perfectly well why me liking you too much is a bad idea.

THEMA   No, I don't.

GWEN   Thema, I'm just not up for anymore rejection so soon after Betsy.

THEMA   *(This takes immense courage.)*   Who says I'd reject you?

(Pause.)

GWEN   You don't mean that.

THEMA   Would I say something like that if I didn't mean it?

(Silence.)

THEMA   Please don't stare. That wasn't easy for me to say.

GWEN   But you didn't want to have anything to do with me after I tried to kiss you that time.

THEMA   We used to kiss each other all the time.

GWEN   Not with our mouths open.

THEMA   But I wanted to. That's probably why I ran. You were a lot braver than I was.

GWEN   Not brave. Crazy.

THEMA   I was so unhappy married. Every marriage I was sure was going to be wonderful. And they never were. I'd go shopping and see you and Betsy together, and I'd feel sad for days. It took me years to finally figure out why; to face what I'd let go by.

GWEN   What?

THEMA   Happiness.

GWEN   But you wouldn't've been.

THEMA   What?

GWEN   Happy. You wouldn't've been. When you were sixteen, you wanted to be Betty Crocker Homemaker of the Year. You didn't wanna be queer, you wanted to go to the prom. You wanted to be Normal. Hell, you wouldn't've been happy with me, you would've been miserable. We'd've done it once and you'd've hated me for doing that to you. It's the truth.

THEMA   Maybe. But it's yesterday's truth. I'm talking about today, right now.

(Sister enters.)

SISTER   I look and I look and there's nothing but closed doors.

THEMA   I know how she feels.

GWEN   *(Used to not talking in front of people, even someone as senile as Sister.)* Thee. *(She shakes her head to indicate she doesn't want to talk about "it" in front of someone.)* Hello, Flora! How you doin'?

SISTER   I need to find a place to spend the night.

GWEN   You've got a place, Flora! You Live Here!

THEMA   Who won the game, Aunt Flora? Who won the card game?

SISTER   I need to find a place to spend the night! *(She exits.)*

GWEN   Well, I guess she told us.

(Grandma enters.)

GRANDMA   Oh. I thought Sister might be here.

THEMA You just missed her. She went thataway. *(She points.)*

GRANDMA She actually won that game. Either she was in an awfully bright mood, or I'm slipping.

THEMA Don't say that.

GWEN You just wore yourself out spooning on the porch with that widower.

GRANDMA Oh, Gwen, I was not.

GWEN Well, why not? I thought he was kind of cute. Not my type, but cute.

GRANDMA You know, he is awfully clean. I appreciate that in a man. Thema's grandfather got so he just wouldn't bathe when he was Mr. Lindberg's age. Oh, he just reeked. And he was so clean when he was young. He was neat as a pin. But once he got old, he was a handful. He'd lie awake all night and smoke in bed, one right after the other, and I'd lie awake, too, just terrified he was going to burn us up.

GWEN Does Mr. Lindberg smoke?

THEMA When he's around Grandma he does.

GRANDMA Oh, you two girls are terrible.

(The phone rings.)

THEMA I'll get it.

GRANDMA Thank you, dear. I think I'll just go check on Sister.

THEMA *(Picks up the phone.)* Hello.

GRANDMA She's a little like having a child around. You don't want to let her out of your sight for too long. Is that for me, Thema?

(Thema shakes her head no.)

GRANDMA I'll be right back. *(She exits.)*

THEMA *(Into the phone.)* Yes; she told me you called. *(Pause.)*

No, I haven't been trying to get ahold of you. Rule, this may come as a surprise to you, but I left you a couple weeks ago. *(Pause.)* No, I Don't want to come home. I have no intention of coming home. *(Pause.)* Rule, be civil or I'm hangin' up this phone. *(Pause.)* No, I don't want to see you. In fact, as soon as I get the money together I'm going to see a lawyer and divorce you, that's how much I don't want to see you. *(Pause.)* No, I do not miss that. I especially don't miss that. *(She hangs up. She and Gwen look at each other.)*

GWEN I gather that was Rule.

THEMA Roaring drunk.

GWEN Do you think he'll come over here?

THEMA God, I hope not, but he might. I'm supposed to go to work in a couple of hours, but I hate to leave them here alone in case he does.

GWEN I could sleep over tonight. *(Immediately afraid Thema might misinterpret.)* I could sleep down here on the couch while you're gone. I'd be glad to tell that son-of-a-bitch what I think of him if he comes over.

THEMA You'd do that?

GWEN Sure. That's what friends are for.

(She and Thema look at each other.)

GWEN Why don't I run home, get my pajamas and a change of clothes, feed the cats, let the dog out, and come back? I'll make sure I get back before you leave.

THEMA You're sure . . .

GWEN *(Finishes for her.)* I wouldn't mind.

THEMA Thank you.

GWEN Don't mention it. I mean that. *(She smiles.)* I'll be back in an hour. *(She exits.)*

THEMA Rule I marry, her I run away from. Jesus.

Scene 5

(It's early Sunday morning. Gwen is still asleep on the couch. Thema enters. She stands and looks at Gwen sleeping. She moves closer, leans down, touches Gwen's shoulder.)

THEMA   Gwen? Honey?

GWEN   *(Groggy, two thirds asleep.)*   Bets? Besty? What time is it? What am I doing on the   *(Realization.)*   couch? Morning.

THEMA   Morning.

GWEN   You just getting in from work?

THEMA   Uh hmm. I hated to wake you, but Grandma and Aunt Flora will be up soon. Grandma likes to watch all the church services on TV full blast. How'd you sleep?

GWEN   *(She pulls away her blanket, sits up. She's fully dressed except for shoes.)*   Oh, pretty good. Finally.

THEMA   Rule was here.

GWEN   You saw the door?

THEMA   No, I just see you're dressed—what door?

GWEN   He kicked in the front door.

THEMA   Oh, no. Goddammit. What happened? What did you do?

GWEN   I went out on the porch and told him he owed Pansy a new door.

THEMA   How'd he take that?

GWEN   I think he was so shocked seeing me out there in my pajamas, he didn't know what to say. He just stood there in a stupor 'til I went back inside. Then he started pounding on the house, yelling for you to come out. Which struck me funny.

THEMA   *(Doesn't get it.)*   Why?

GWEN   Him wanting you to come out. Never mind. Why don't you go on up to bed? I should put on my shoes and get going. My cats are probably starving—or think they are. I put my clothes back on after he was here. I didn't like dealing with that guy in my pajamas.

THEMA   Did it scare Grandma and Sister?

GWEN   Well, Flora was afraid the Germans had landed, but Pansy took it in her stride. She said it was just a door. She was just glad he didn't hurt anybody.

THEMA   He could have.

GWEN   But he didn't.

THEMA   What if he'd hit you?

GWEN   I would've hit him back.

THEMA   *(Starting to cry.)*   Oh, God, I've made such a mess of things. What if you'd been hurt?

GWEN   *(Shyly moves to hold her.)*   But I wasn't. Everything's okay. I'll tell my brother to talk to Rule. He'll never cross Arnie. My baby brother's about the size of that couch. Oh, Thee, don't. Everything's all right.   *(She strokes Thema's back.)*   I'm just glad you're not living with that asshole any more.

(They stand holding each other for a moment longer. Then they hear slow, hesitating steps on the stairs. They look at each other for a moment, then, self-consciously, separate.)

THEMA   You're so dear.

GWEN   You should get some sleep.

THEMA   Will you be here when I get up?

GWEN   I have to go home to let out my dog. Feed my cats.

THEMA   How long does that take?

GWEN   I can come back in the late afternoon if you like.

THEMA   Come for dinner?

GWEN   You know, Thee, I'd come over even if you didn't feed me.

THEMA   I like feeding you.

GWEN   You're going to spoil me.

THEMA   You're spoiling Me.

GWEN At the moment, I'm keeping you up. Why don't you go on up to bed? I'll be back in a bit.

THEMA Please. Come back.

GWEN Twist my arm.

THEMA If I have to.

(Grandma and Sister finally enter—they take their time climbing stairs. Sister wanders here and there, bewildered. It's all new to her. Occasionally, she'll count as if to reassure herself.)

GRANDMA Good morning, girls. Isn't it a beautiful morning?

GWEN Beautiful, Pansy.

SISTER 12, 14, 16, 18.

THEMA Gwen's coming back for supper, Grandma. What would you think about grilling steaks?

GRANDMA Now, Thema, you know I can't chew a steak.

THEMA All right, then, we'll just grill us some hamburgers. Now, I know you can chew a hamburger.

GRANDMA Are you sure you know how to operate that thing? Horace was the last person to operate it.

THEMA Sounds like we might need a fresh bag of charcoal. Grandpa's been dead since 1953.

GRANDMA I'm so teetery, I'm afraid I'd fall right in the fire if I tried to operate it.

GWEN Don't worry, Pansy. I'm an expert. I love to grill.

THEMA See. Now you have to come.

GWEN I'll even bring the hamburger.

THEMA Good.

GWEN And potato chips. Pansy, you tell her to go to bed, will you? See you all later. *(She exits.)*

SISTER 2, 4, 6, 8.

THEMA *(Intones.)* Who do we appreciate. That was an old high school cheer. Gwen would remember. *(Yawns.)*

GRANDMA You do look tired, Thema.

THEMA Well, you probably are, too. I'm sorry about Rule. Sounds like he really raised hell.

GRANDMA That's over and done with. Don't you lose any sleep over it.

THEMA If I'm not up by four, rap on the ceiling with the broom, will you? Good night. Or good evening. Whatever. *(She exits.)*

GRANDMA Sleep tight.

SISTER 3, 4, 3, 4, 3, 4.

GRANDMA Your record's stuck, Sister.

SISTER I'm scared, and I'm lost, and I'm frightened. It's so steep up here. *(Abruptly, she stops walking, blinded by a shaft of early morning light shining through the window.)* Oh, I'm blinded. I can't see a thing. *(Swaying slightly in front of the window.)* Don't let me fall. Mama, please don't let me fall.

GRANDMA You're all right, Sister.

SISTER Mama?

GRANDMA No, Sister, Mama's been dead since 1918. It's Pansy. Why don't you sit down, Flora. You're making me dizzy swaying like that.

SISTER I got myself up here on this mountaintop, and I can't get down.

GRANDMA *(Rising slowly, stiffly, from her chair.)* Oh, dear, and my head's just swimming. Just stand there for a minute, sweetheart. I'll help you down. I'll be right there. *(She slowly reels toward Sister.)*

SISTER I've always been scared of heights. I couldn't even go up in the haymow when I was a child.

GRANDMA I remember.

SISTER Just looking up at that haymow made me dizzy. And now here I've gotten myself stranded on a mountaintop, and all I was trying to do was find my way home.

GRANDMA *(One hand clasping the back of a chair for balance, she grasps Sister's forearm with her other hand.)* Here, Sister. I've got you. You're safe now. Turn away from the window. It's just a window, Sister. *(She slowly turns her, maneuvers her the few steps to a chair, sits her down.)* There. You're safe now.

SISTER Phew. Phew. That was a close one. I almost lost me that time.

(Grandma slowly inches her way back to the safety of her own chair.)

GRANDMA My. That wore me right out.

(Thema enters in pajamas, toothbrush in hand.)

THEMA Is everything all right? I thought I heard quite a ruckus down here.

GRANDMA Oh, we just had to rescue Sister from the mountaintop.

THEMA Oh.

GRANDMA It was a tall order.

THEMA Well, if everything's okay, I guess I'll get to bed. Would you like the TV on, Gram? It must be about time for your shows.

GRANDMA Why it is. It's almost eight o'clock and we haven't even eaten our breakfast yet. Turn it to Channel 33, would you? That's Oral Roberts. I hope he hasn't blessed all the crippled people yet. I just love to watch the wheelchair section start rolling toward the pulpit.

THEMA *(Turning on the TV.)* Boy, am I sorry I'm gonna miss that. Have a good time. *(She exits.)*

(Sister stands.)

GRANDMA Oh, Sister, stay and watch with me.

SISTER I've got to find a place to spend the night.

GRANDMA Oh, Sister, you aren't going to start that again, are you? This is your home. For as long as I live. Share my home with me, Sister.

SISTER I have to find a room before I freeze to death sleeping in this car.

GRANDMA   Sit and watch the program, Sister. You can find a room later. Evening's a long way off, Sister.

SISTER   I ate a rat once. Killed it with a shovel.

GRANDMA   I believe you told me that one, honey.

SISTER   You ever gutted a rat?

Scene 6

(Grandma is napping in her chair. No one else is around. Gwen enters with a bag of groceries. She looks around, checks her watch, frowns, sets down the groceries and walks over to Grandma. She touches her shoulder gently, then more firmly.)

GWEN   Pansy, Pansy?

GRANDMA   What? Oh, Gwen. Why you're back already. My that was fast.

GWEN   Honey, it's nearly five o'clock. How long have you been napping?

GRANDMA   Five o'clock? Oh, my, I guess I did nap.

GWEN   Well, none of us slept very well with Rule out on the porch raising a fuss. You were probably making up for last night.

GRANDMA   Isn't Thema up yet? Oh, dear, I promised to make sure she was up by four. You must think we're an awfully lazy family.

GWEN   I think you're a wonderful family.

GRANDMA   Where's Sister? Did you see her when you came in?

GWEN   No. Maybe she's upstairs in her room. I'll run up and check.

GRANDMA   Would you mind? I worry if I've let her out of my sight for too long.

GWEN   I'll check upstairs.

GRANDMA   And tap on Thema's door, will you?

GWEN   Sure, I'll be glad to. Now don't worry.   *(She exits.)*

GRANDMA   *(Talking to herself.)*   I just hope she hasn't gone looking for a hotel.   *(Hands on her armrests, she rocks a couple of times, finally rocking herself to her feet.)*   Maybe she's in the bathroom. *(She starts slowly across the room, leaning on furniture as she goes.)*   Maybe she's back to looking for her geese in there. Though where she got the idea we have geese I just don't know. And what would they be doing in the bathroom? *(She exits.)*

(A moment later, Gwen enters, empty-handed. Thema, tying her robe, follows.)

GWEN   Great. Now we've lost Pansy.

THEMA   Grandma? Grandma!

(Grandma re-enters, flustered.)

GRANDMA   The basement door is open. Sister knocks at that door when she's looking for a room, but she usually can't work the latch. But the door's open.

GWEN   Thema, help her back to her chair. I'll check the basement.

THEMA   Grandma, it's going to be all right. Everything's all right.

(Gwen exits. Thema looks after her.)

GRANDMA   But what if she's fallen? What if she's fallen?

THEMA   Well, then, we'll deal with it, Gram. We'll deal with it together.

Scene 7

(It's night. Gwen is sitting alone. Thema enters from upstairs.)

THEMA   I finally got her to bed.

GWEN   She probably won't sleep very well though. She's gonna be worried about Flora's surgery tomorrow morning.

THEMA Do you think she'll make it?

GWEN She may. She may. She's got a strong heart.

THEMA But she probably won't walk again with that pin in her hip.

GWEN Let's take that on when it comes. If it comes.

THEMA Grandma's just beside herself.

GWEN Old age is no treat. Too much of it's waiting to see what you break next.

THEMA Well, we've still got a little time left.

GWEN Yes.

THEMA I'm sorry we didn't get to grill those hamburgers.

GWEN We'll do it another time.

THEMA I hope so.

(Pause.)

THEMA I know. Your dog's gotta pee and your cats are hungry.

GWEN Well, actually, I fed the cats before I left, and I left my dog out, just in case Rule decide to drop by. I don't think he will, but if he does he'll get a greeting he'll never forget.

THEMA Is your brother going to talk to him?

GWEN He already did. I told him it could wait 'til tomorrow, but he got pretty steamed when he heard about what happened. He drove right over to your place—Rule's place—and read him the riot act. Told him he expected him to send Pansy money to pay for that door he kicked in. And he told Rule if he even looked cross-eyed at you or me, he'd pulverize him. Arnie thinks Rule got the message, but it's hard to know how sensible he'll be after another night of drinking.

THEMA I sure can pick 'em, can't I?

GWEN You left him, Thee. Don't carry him around with you.

THEMA I don't want to. God, I don't want to.

GWEN It is hard not to. I know.

THEMA   Will you ever . . . ?

GWEN   Ever what?

THEMA   Stop carrying Betsy around with you?

GWEN   I don't know. I honestly don't. She came along at a time in my life when I thought I'd always be alone. Having her want to be with me made me feel comfortable with myself for the first time in my life. I got spoiled. The years went by, and I knew she wasn't as content as I was, but I just didn't know what to say that would make her stay. I was still so amazed she'd stayed in the first place.

THEMA   I guess that answers my question.

GWEN   Sure I still carry her around. But I'm a strong woman. I can carry all sorts of things at once.

THEMA   I'm glad. Do you still hear from her?

GWEN   A postcard now and then. Something arty, so I can see how much she's enjoying living someplace cultured.

THEMA   I can't imagine leaving you for New York City.

GWEN   You left me for Art Underwood.

THEMA   I left you, because you scared me.

GWEN   Did I?

THEMA   I was so attracted to you it scared the shit out of me.

GWEN   Oh.

THEMA   I wish you'd say more than oh.

GWEN   What do you want me to say?

THEMA   Gwen, you've been on my mind for years. And you're all I've been able to think about the last week or two. I wasted years trying not to reach out to you, and now that's all I want to do.

GWEN   Thee, you just left your husband. Flora's in the hospital. Your world's all upsidedown right now. You're confused. I've been here, and you're grateful . . .

THEMA   Gwen, what I'm feeling isn't gratitude.

GWEN Thee, I don't go after straight women. I just don't.

THEMA Will you tell me one thing?

GWEN If I can.

THEMA What's straight mean?

GWEN I'm sorry. That means heterosexual. You know, boy-boy, girl-girl? I'm gay. I always have been. And I've found that it's more sensible to sleep with other lesbians. They're not so surprised the next day when they wake up next to a woman.

THEMA You never used to be so damn sensible.

GWEN Old age.

THEMA Gwen, aren't you even a little bit interested in me?

GWEN I guess maybe now you scare me.

THEMA And it all boils down to something I wouldn't do with you when I was a kid. God, I'm tired of living in the past, aren't you? Do you want to spend the rest of your life alone?

GWEN Maybe.

THEMA You do not. And neither do I.

GWEN Thema, you don't even know if you'd like it.

THEMA What?

GWEN Well, you know.

THEMA Sex. Having sex with you.

GWEN You can't talk to me about forever and ever and not even be sure if you'd like it.

THEMA Do you have to keep calling it "it"?

GWEN Thema, please. No jokes.

THEMA Gwen, what I really want and need is love. If the sex is good, that's a bonus. I've always loved you. And I think you're still kind of fond of me or I wouldn't make you so nervous.

GWEN Thee, if we ever *(Brief pause.)* got together, I'd want it to last.

THEMA So would I.

GWEN You don't know the crap there is in being the town dyke.

THEMA Oh, honey, my reputation's been drug through the mud so many times, being with you wouldn't do a thing to it.

GWEN There's a lot of pleasure in loving women, but it doesn't stay private in a town like this. Could you face Everyone knowing? You couldn't when we were kids.

THEMA Hell, Rule probably figures we've already been to bed. He's pretty slow, but he did see you here in your pajamas.

GWEN He did holler he's twice the man I am a couple times. But you know he'll never tell. How would that make him look? It'd make him look like he's not as good as I am.

THEMA Are you good?

GWEN Well, I'd lay odds I'm better'n he is. Hell, my dog's probably better in bed than Rule is.

THEMA I'm not interested in your dog.

GWEN Thema, are you sure?

THEMA Honest to God, I'm not interested in your dog.

GWEN Thee.

THEMA Do you want me to court you? Should I bring you candy and flowers? I don't know how it's done. Is that how it's done?

GWEN That'd be nice, but you don't need to.

THEMA I never had to court my husbands. I never wanted to. I've never wanted to court anyone but you.

GWEN I thought life, this part of it, ended when Betsy left.

THEMA You're still striking. My husbands you could take in all at one glance. I could just look at you for hours and always be seeing something new.

GWEN May I kiss you?

THEMA I wish you would.

GWEN Are you sure?

THEMA   No. But I think it's time we gave it another try.

(Gwen leans in, hesitantly, kisses her briefly. Thema kisses Gwen. This is a longer kiss.)

THEMA   You can't know what a pleasure it is to kiss someone who doesn't taste like tobacco juice.

GWEN   I love you, Thee. I always have.

THEMA   God, honey, I love you, too. Will you come upstairs with me?

GWEN   Thee, are you sure?

THEMA   *(Looks momentarily vulnerable.)*   No. But I think we've waited just about long enough.

GWEN   Jesus, now I'm gonna get performance anxiety.

THEMA   Well, you are bound to be better than Rule. He never even bothered to take his socks off.

GWEN   He Was bad if you were looking at his feet.

(Thema turns to walk up the stairs, looks back over her shoulder, extends a hand toward Gwen.)

THEMA   Are you coming?

GWEN   I guess I am.

(They exit.)

Scene 8

(Gwen and Grandma are sitting in the living room. Gwen is massaging Grandma's lower leg.)

GWEN   That better?

GRANDMA   Yes. Oh, yes, that cramp's completely gone now. You've got wonderful hands, Gwen.

GWEN   So I've been told.

(The back door opens, closes. Thema enters.)

THEMA   She made it.

GRANDMA   Thank God.

GWEN   Terrific.

THEMA   She's going to be unconscious for a few hours, so I thought I'd run home and tell you rather than call. They said her vital signs are all good.

GRANDMA   I just hope I'm not being selfish wanting her to live like I do.

THEMA   Selfish? Oh, come on, Grandma. You wouldn't know how to be selfish.

GRANDMA   My brother, Laurence, had an expression, "Sometimes the ambulance gets there too soon." You know, instead of it getting there too late, it gets there too soon? Sometimes it is better for people if you let them die.

GWEN   But, honey, it's not up to you or us, it's up to Flora, and apparently she's still got the will to live. You wouldn't want to wish her dead until she's ready to go.

GRANDMA   But what if she can't get so she can walk again? She'll have to go in the Home, won't she? She'll have to go to the Home. And she and I always promised we'd never let that happen to each other.

THEMA   She doesn't have to go in the Home, Gram. I'm here. I can help you take care of her.

GWEN   I can, too, Pansy. There's no reason Flora has to go to the Home. No reason at all. We'll all take care of her here.

THEMA   *(Quietly.)*   Do you mean that?

GWEN   Absolutely.

GRANDMA   You two are just the best girls in the world.

THEMA   Well, we love Aunt Flora, too, Gram. We want her to finish out her life here, where she belongs.

GRANDMA   Oh, I'm so relieved. Now I can go eat something.

(They laugh. Grandma rocks in her chair a couple of times to build up the momentum to eject herself.)

GWEN You need a hand, Pansy?

GRANDMA Oh, no. I can still stand up on my own. It just takes longer than it used to. *(She rocks to her feet.)* There.

THEMA There's some leftover meatloaf for a sandwich. Or I could make you some eggs . . .

GRANDMA I think I'm just going to eat some cereal and then go upstairs for a nice long nap. Do you work tonight, Thema?

THEMA No, but I want to go back to the hospital in an hour or so to check on Aunt Flora. I want to be there when she wakes up.

GRANDMA *(Slowly reeling her way across the room.)* Give her my love. Tell her she's in my thoughts and prayers.

GWEN You can tell her I'm counting for her.

GRANDMA My, it is strange not to hear that, isn't it? I miss Sister desperately, but I can do without that counting. *(Exiting.)* I'll see you girls in a bit. *(She exits.)*

(Pause.)

GWEN Hi.

THEMA Hi.

GWEN How you doing?

THEMA Fine. How about you?

GWEN I'm kinda happy myself.

THEMA You look happy.

GWEN Any regrets?

THEMA You bet.

GWEN Oh. *(Brief pause.)* I guess I should've expected you might have.

THEMA Not those kind of regrets, honey. I'm just sorry it took all these years. *(Touching Gwen.)* I'm very happy about us.

GWEN Maybe it's good it took us so long. Now we've got the sense to value what we have.

THEMA I'm really looking forward to this.

GWEN This what?

THEMA Life.

GWEN So am I.

CURTAIN

HANNAH FREE

Cast of Characters

Hannah   a feisty old lesbian confined to a nursing home

Rachel   her comatose lover down the hall; a nonspeaking role

Rachel   the spirit of the younger Rachel; she visits Hannah

Greta   Hannah's other visitor

Marge   Rachel's daughter and prison warden

Nurse

Mail Lady

Old Man

Minister

Setting

Yesterday and today; reality and memory; a nursing home and elsewhere.

Notes

Feel free to double cast the smaller parts.

A 1992 premiere at Bailiwick Repertory in Chicago; Laurie Attea, director; Lauren Love, assistant director.

Summary

Hannah Free is the story of Hannah, an independent spirit, and Rachel, the homebody she loves all her life. The play opens in a nursing home where an elderly Hannah is not allowed to see a comatose Rachel who is just down the hall. Denied Rachel, Hannah visits with Rachel's spirit, and they bicker and remember the love that began when they were just girls, sitting together in school. *Hannah Free* is a fiction about all the real women who've loved each other for decades and decades. It's a story about living and loving and letting go.

Author's Note

Few plays are written about elderly lesbians. Fewer plays deal with their extreme vulnerability in a system that doesn't recognize our rights. I wanted to deal with those issues while also creating a love story about two women who loved each other for decades despite a few flaws and more than a few differences.

ACT I

Scene 1

(Hannah Free is sitting up in bed in her room at the nursing home. A nurse enters with medicine and juice from her medication cart.)

NURSE   You gonna get up today, Hannah?   *(She hands Hannah a cup of juice and a pill in a smaller cup.)*

HANNAH   *(Suspicious.)*   What's this?

NURSE   That's orange juice, Hannah.

HANNAH   *(Triumphant.)*   Don'tcha know I'm allergic to Vitamin C?

NURSE   *(Frowns.)*   Is that on your chart?

HANNAH   How the hell do I know? It's supposed to be.

NURSE   You're sure you're allergic to Vitamin C?

(Hannah gives her belligerent silence for an answer. She is Not senile.)

NURSE   Well, better safe than sorry I always say. Let's give you a little milk instead.   *(She goes out to the hall to her cart to pour the milk.)*

HANNAH   We go through this about every other week, but it's always news to her.

NURSE   *(Returning with the milk.)*   Wouldn't you like to get dressed today and eat with the others?

HANNAH   I wanna see Rachel. You let me see Rachel I'll go sit with those basket cases down the hall.

NURSE   Now Hannah, Rachel's very sick.

HANNAH   I know she's sick goddammit.

NURSE   Only her family can see her.

HANNAH   I'm family.

NURSE   Now don't get all ruffled or we'll have to give you something. You know your blood pressure.

HANNAH   You tell Marge I wanna see her mother.

NURSE   All right, Hannah, I'll tell her. But I told her day before yesterday and she said no; it would just upset you both.

HANNAH   Rachel's gonna die alone!

NURSE   Now Hannah, her daughter comes to see her every day.

HANNAH   But Rachel needs to see Me.

NURSE   She must be an old friend isn't she?

HANNAH   All our lives. Friend doesn't begin to say it. Please. I'll get up. I'll let you dress and powder me. I'll even eat with those corpses in your diningroom if you'll just let me see her.

NURSE   You let the nurse's aide dress you and eat a good lunch. Then we'll see.

HANNAH   It would mean a lot to both of us.

NURSE   *(Exiting.)*   Well, that's what we want. That's what we're here for.   *(Exits.)*

HANNAH   *(To audience.)*   Can you imagine? Doing That for a living? Then she'll end up in here herself when she's eighty. They finally got me last winter when I broke my hip shoveling snow off the garage roof, but Jesus God you sure wouldn'ta caught me here when I was her age. She oughta get herself a job outside. People nowadays are indoors too much—who can breathe? Those big office buildings you can't even look out a window. Same air's been circulatin' since 1940 only now there's more dead pigeons in the air filters. It's no way to live. At least this room's got a view and a window that opens. I fought 'em 'til they moved me to this side of the building where I can see the woods and the railroad tracks. There's a freight goes by at two every morning. I listen for it. I'd kill myself or somebody else if all I could see was parking lot. That's all Rachel sees from her room. Not that she sees. Well, why the hell should she open her eyes? Who'd wanna see This place?

(The delightful mail lady enters.)

MAIL LADY   Good morning, Hannah. You got some mail this morning. I know I saw something in here . . . another postcard. . .   *(Sings out.)*   Here it is! All the way from Alaska.

Look at the size of that fish. It's a *(Reads description on the back.)* halibut. *(She points at the picture. The postcard is just out of Hannah's reach.)* Will you look at that. 356 pounds. How do they even catch a thing like that? Can you imagine going for a swim and seeing That in the water with you? No thanks. Here, would you like me to read it to you?

(Hannah frowns, extends her hand for it. Mail Lady doesn't notice Hannah's hand. She continues in her delightful way.)

MAIL LADY   That's all right. I'll just read it to you like I usually do.

(Hannah scowls, sinks back in disgust. Oblivious, the Mail Lady reads on.)

MAIL LADY   It says, "Hey, Hannah. The mud got another one. Love and regards, Nettie Bobo." I wonder what that means? Do you have any idea what that means?

(Hannah just ignores her. She can't stand her.)

MAIL LADY   *(Drops card in Hannah's lap.)*   Well, gotta go. See you tomorrow, hon. *(Hannah flinches.)* That's some fish. My hubby would sell his soul to hook into a fish like that. Alaska. How do you know somebody in Alaska? *(She exits talking.)*

HANNAH   Isn't it enough to be old? Isn't it enough I'm crippled up so bad I can't walk? It's people like that drive people like me nuts. Trap us like rats and then talk us to death. I can't just walk away like I used to. That was my signature. I didn't like somethin', off I'd go. That's how I ended up in Alaska. Taught school at Barrow. No roads. Everybody flew. I flew over that tundra like it was my backyard. Millions of square miles of backyard. Nettie's still there. *(Indicates postcard.)* 92. Canoes to work. Digs tourists out of the mudflats. They think they're out for a stroll on the beach only it's not beach. They sink down in that ooze and stick like cement. Tide comes in, you're history. *(Indicates card.)* "The mud got another one." I loved it there. But I had to come back. Always had to come back. For Rachel. She'd never leave Michigan. She always had those damn kids. And peaches to can and pies to bake. She'd look like somebody dipped her in flour. She looked a little bit like Mt. McKinley.

(A young Rachel, streaked with flour, appears.)

RACHEL   I like that. Being compared to a mountain.

HANNAH It was a compliment.

RACHEL You were gone so long I thought you were never coming back.

HANNAH You got married.

RACHEL To escape my father's temper, not you. I had to get away.

HANNAH And girls are Supposed to marry.

RACHEL At least I married Mr. Johnson, the dullest man I could find. The only person I ever knew who felt compelled to sit in the outhouse and read each page of the Sears Roebuck before he'd use it.

HANNAH He was a good provider, but you would've been trapped for life.

RACHEL If Mr. Johnson hadn't had the misfortune of dying on that excursion boat.

HANNAH Everyone ran to one side of the boat to wave goodbye and the boat capsized. Twenty people drowned not twenty feet from the dock. What was a dull person like him doing on an excursion boat in the first place, her pregnant with twins? Never marry a weak swimmer.

RACHEL It was nearly dark at the time of the accident. Men jumped in after them, saved a few, probably the loudest, the shouters. But many died, weighted down by wet party clothes. After an hour someone brought a lumber hook and they hooked a few, but in the dark many bodies were taken by the lake, swallowed whole. I rowed the shoreline every day until I saw him bobbing in the lilypads at the far end of the lake. Some boys out frogging tied a rope to him so I could haul him in for proper burial.

HANNAH You waited months to write me, 'til after the twins were born. You read your Bible and prayed. Fought with yourself. And you tried to mourn him. But it was always me you wanted to cook for.

RACHEL Don't be smug. *(Brief pause.)* You used to wear that black velveteen dress to school. I was envious. We'd sit on the recitation bench together and I'd admire the fabric so much I'd lose my place. Gradually I realized it wasn't the dress I admired.

HANNAH She always thought we were the only two girls who did
   what we did. And believe me, we did it whenever and
   wherever we could. But after it was over, she'd make me
   leave the chicken coop or the haymow and she'd read her
   Bible. It never seemed to be on my side and neither did her
   father. Miserable old s.o.b.

RACHEL Well he's dead now.

HANNAH But she's still got people. Her daughter sits with her
   hour after hour and won't let me see her. Even has the nerve
   to say it's for my own good. How seein' her wasted away to
   sixty pounds might kill me. Kill me, Jesus. I've done all I was
   meant to. I'd like to take one look at her 'n die. That's be a
   nice way to go.

RACHEL Isn't this a switch? For once you're staying in one spot
   and I'm the one leaving. If they'll just let me.

HANNAH I had to go; I had to see things.

RACHEL Alaska. New Mexico. Paris. My Lord even Ohio. Why
   Ohio? It's Michigan only flat.

HANNAH Some of Ohio is Very pretty. You've never seen it.

RACHEL Every so often she just had to leave me. She knew I'd be
   wild for her when she finally got back.

HANNAH I've been everywhere. Even South America. That's
   where I found the seeds for her moonflowers.

RACHEL My late husband used to walk with his eyes on the
   ground like he was always looking for lost change. He
   wouldn't have known a day lily from a lilac bush. What do
   wives find to talk about with husbands? Mr. Johnson and I
   ran out of conversation in less than two years.

HANNAH She and I both love flowers and I'd just never seen
   anything like those moonflowers. They'd come out at dusk
   with the moon and then they'd unfold in seconds 'til they
   were the prettiest yellow flowers, like yellow morning glories.
   Her little girl would beg to stay up with us, and we'd sit in
   lawnchairs watching those flowers open like we were
   watching a fireworks display. We'd ooh and ah and point.
   Then it was over and the mosquitos would drive us inside. I'd
   carry her daughter upstairs and put her to bed 'cause by then
   she was asleep. Then maybe I'd get to stay; maybe I wouldn't.
   I used to call Rachel my moonflower when I was pressing up

under her nightgown. But by morning both her and the moonflowers would shrivel up and have their hairnets back on.

RACHEL   How was I supposed to cook breakfast without a hairnet?

HANNAH   But you had such beautiful hair. I hated seeing it all held back like that.

RACHEL   Hannah, don't start anything we can't finish.

(Rachel's daughter, Marge, enters. Rachel steps to one side and watches. Marge can't see her.)

MARGE   *(Speaking loudly.)*   Hello, Hannah!

HANNAH   Marge, I can hear. Just can't walk or see worth a shit.

RACHEL   But you do see me.

MARGE   The nurse says you've been wanting to see Mom.

HANNAH   Of course I have.

MARGE   We can't have you upsetting her.

HANNAH   Upset? Upset?! When have I ever upset your mother?

MARGE   All her life.

HANNAH   Well, if that's true it was by choice. Her choice as well as mine. Let me see her, Marge. We need to see each other. This is no way to end our lives, three doors away but alone.

MARGE   She has her family.   *(Turns to leave.)*

HANNAH   *(Anguished.)*   I'm her family!

MARGE   Please, Hannah. Don't.

HANNAH   I used to tuck you in. Told you stories. I'd sit up with you if there was a storm. You never knew your father, but you knew me. You knew I'd always look after you.

MARGE   *(A bit of childish resentment creeps in.)*   When you weren't busy in Alaska or New Mexico.

HANNAH   I sent you postcards. I sent you presents. I sent your mother money. How the hell do you think you ate during the Depression?

MARGE Don't act like you were always there for Mom. You weren't. We were. Roy and I were there.

HANNAH Dammit you were children. You Had to be there.

MARGE Hannah, I grew up a long time ago. I lost a daughter in a car accident. I have grown grandchildren. I cook, I clean, I can peaches and recycle my newspapers. Maybe once a year we drive up to the Mackinac Bridge *(pronounced Mackinaw)* and I get to eat fudge by the water. Then we come home and I mow the lawn. I'm busy, Hannah. I have a life. But when she needs me I come. You came when you darn well pleased.

HANNAH You just don't know anything about it.

MARGE I'll tell Mom you asked after her. She won't hear, but I'll tell her. *(She exits.)*

HANNAH She was a cute little girl, but she's been a pain in the ass ever since she joined the Baptist Church. *(Yells at door.)* Save your judgments, Marge! Save 'em for somebody who'll listen!

RACHEL Marge used to like to sleep with me. When you came over, it made her jealous to sleep in her own bed. I wonder if she remembers. You read me that Greek play where the boy kills his father then accidentally marries his mother. There's a lot of that kind of thing in real life, only it's subtle.

(A young woman, Greta, enters.)

GRETA Hi. Are you Grandma Hannah?

HANNAH What?!

GRETA The nurse said I should talk to "Grandma Hannah" about my project for school.

HANNAH Stop calling me that. Jesus Christ.

GRETA I'm sorry. I guess she . . .

HANNAH *(Interrupting.)* Well, what? The Depression? Women's Suffrage? The Civil War? What d'ya need my sage words about I'm busy.

GRETA The Depression.

HANNAH I went to Alaska. Caught everything I ate except chocolate. Didn't need money so I mailed my pay home to a friend with children. When the War came, I lied about my age, joined the WACs, and fought the War in New Mexico. In the Fifties, I invested in computer stocks and that's how come a Depression rat like me can afford this beauteous private suite at Hotel Hell. I voted for Roosevelt because I liked Eleanor. That's it. Posterity.

GRETA   You get asked this a lot.

HANNAH   No kiddin'. I'm the only coherent old fart in this place. They send alla you in here like you'll perk me up. What the hell am I? The public library? Go ask your parents what it was like growing up in 1960.

GRETA   My parents are dead.

HANNAH   Well, so are mine.

(They glare at each other for a moment, then laugh.)

GRETA   What an awful place.

HANNAH   Always keep a gun handy to shoot yourself if you ever break a hip. Now up in Alaska if I'da fell offa roof a bear woulda ate me and got some use outa me.

GRETA   You've really been to Alaska?

HANNAH   I lived in Alaska. Look here.   *(Shows her the postcard.)* This is from a frienda mine who still lives up there.

RACHEL   Lord, now you're robbing the cradle. I thought I'd seen it all.

HANNAH   *(Glares over at Rachel whom only she hears.)*   Nonsense.

GRETA   Living in Alaska's nonsense?

HANNAH   I'm just mumbling to myself. Old people do that. Naw, Alaska was swell. I was real happy living up there.   *(Gives Rachel a look.)*

GRETA   But how did you survive?

HANNAH   I had my high school diploma, so I taught school. Skinned things. You get by.

GRETA   I admire you. You just went and did it. Most people dream and stay home.

RACHEL   There's nothing wrong with staying home.

GRETA   I'd really love to go to Africa, but I'm afraid I might need a blood transfusion.

HANNAH   Why? Are you sick?

GRETA   No.

HANNAH   Then don't get sick.

GRETA   The blood supply in Africa is so tainted with AIDS . . . what if something Did happen?

HANNAH   God forbid something should happen in your life. Trust me, kiddo, you can "what if" yourself into a pretty boring life.

GRETA   Wow, that's a great philosophy.

RACHEL   I really don't care to watch this.

HANNAH   *(To Rachel.)*   You call this something? I went to your wedding.

GRETA   What?

HANNAH   *(Gestures at the Rachel she sees.)*   She's just being ridiculous. Nothing. Forget it.   *(After a moment of slightly uncomfortable silence.)*   You married?

GRETA   No.

HANNAH   *(Looking Greta over. Talking to herself.)*   I wonder. Hard to tell these days. The girls used to wear a pinky ring. Men's socks.   *(To Greta.)*   How old are you?

GRETA   Twenty.

HANNAH   *(To herself.)*   Well, maybe you don't know yet, but I sure did.

GRETA   Were you ever married?

HANNAH   Not to a man.

GRETA   Oh yeah?

HANNAH   This gonna go in your paper?

GRETA   Maybe. Is she dead?

HANNAH Almost. She's just down the hall. They won't let me see her. She's in a coma, but they still won't let me see her. They're "protecting" us from each other. People were always doing that.

GRETA Is she who you talk to?

HANNAH Since I can't go to her, I bring her to me. I suppose you think that's weird.

GRETA I still talk to my parents. Especially when I can't sleep. You're the only person I've told.

HANNAH Well, I'm pretty damn safe. *(Brief pause, softer tone.)* I won't tell.

GRETA They died last year. Car accident.

HANNAH Rachel's been in a coma about that long. Stroke. It happened when I was in the hospital with this damn hip or I coulda taken care of her. But her "family" had to get involved. That damn daughter. And she's her Legal family, so here I sit.

GRETA And Rachel's just down the hall?

HANNAH Yup. Beats me all to hell what they think I'm going to do to her. I just want to say goodbye.

GRETA That doesn't seem like much to ask.

HANNAH It's like I lost all my goddamn rights. I belong there.

GRETA And her daughter's with her all the time?

HANNAH I think she goes home at night. God, I'm so afraid Rachel's gonna die alone. Late in the night. That'll be her way, to slip away quiet. But I Know if it was up to her she'd want me there.

RACHEL Don't be too sure.

HANNAH *(To Rachel.)* You're So funny. *(To Greta.)* She's being funny.

GRETA A nurse told me they don't lock the front door to the building. People can visit twenty-four hours a day if they want to.

HANNAH Nobody wants to.

GRETA But they can. I mean, I could. Come by around three in the morning and take you for a stroll. Down the hall.

HANNAH *(After a brief pause for the offer to sink in.)* You'd have to help me out of bed and into my chair. How's your back?

GRETA Don't worry, I'm in great shape. I play a lot of softball in the summer, basketball in the winter.

HANNAH *(Nods as if Greta has just ridden by her on a float at a gay pride parade.)* Un Huh.

GRETA So it's no problem.

HANNAH Good, 'cause she could go next year; she could go tonight. I don't wanna miss her.

GRETA Then let's do it tonight. Three o'clock? *(Moves to exit.)*

HANNAH How come? How come you're goin' outa your way for me, kid?

GRETA I don't know. Maybe so somebody'll help me out when I get old.

HANNAH Don't count on it.

(An Old Man wanders in.)

OLD MAN You seen my horses?

HANNAH Nope. All we got in here is goats. Old goats. Check down the hall in the TV room.

OLD MAN All righty, I'll just do that. How the hell'd they get outa the barn, that's what I wanna know. *(Points.)* This way?

HANNAH Take a left at the drinking fountain.

OLD MAN See ya around, toots. *(He winks, exits.)*

GRETA He a regular?

HANNAH Never seen him before. Well, at least he's got all his parts. Those diabetics with stumps for legs just depress the hell outa me. Especially if I used to know'em. Kids I knew in school; now they're up here. It's a strange feeling. They're the real ghosts.

GRETA Is there anything I can bring you? Do you need anything?

HANNAH   Just Rachel.

GRETA   Three o'clock.   *(She shoots a finger at Hannah, exits.)*

HANNAH   Thanks, kiddo.

(Greta exits.)

RACHEL   Well, it's not the first time you've waved somebody under my nose. That missionary followed you all the way from Brazil.

HANNAH   Am I gonna hear about Her again? Ancient history.

RACHEL   All the way from Brazil. Followed you on a banana boat.

HANNAH   Clean food and American toilets were what looked good to her, not me. Everything down there gave her diarrhea.

RACHEL   Why do you have to give Every Little Detail? Good Lord, I do not want to hear about that woman's bathroom habits.

HANNAH   You always were one to pull the curtains.

RACHEL   Some things are private.

HANNAH   You mean hidden. Decades of hiding. Pretending. Your husband's photograph on the mantel and flowers on his grave every Decoration Day. You'd visit with all the other good widows at the cemetery; then you'd come home and crawl back in bed with me.

RACHEL   I can't talk to you. I never could.

HANNAH   But you sure tried.

RACHEL   I'm going back to my room.

HANNAH   Fine.

(Neither moves.)

HANNAH   Used to be we'd make up by doing the deed. I'd keep at you 'til your clothes were off.

RACHEL   That time is long past.

HANNAH   I still feel it. I still want you same as I always did.

RACHEL   Not the way I am now. Down the hall plugged in like a lamp. *(Brief pause.)*   I really don't want you to see.

HANNAH   You'll always be the same to me.

RACHEL   Bull.

HANNAH   Rachel!

RACHEL   Always calling me a prude, but you hate it when I talk as plain as you do. You really want some sweet thing you can strut your stuff for.

HANNAH   It's too bad I never found one.

(More glaring.)

RACHEL   What did I ever see in you?

HANNAH   Beats me.

(Door opens. Nurse enters with enema kit.)

NURSE   Well, it's that time again, Hannah. Let's put you on the toilet.

HANNAH   I haven't eaten anything. I don't need cleaning out if I haven't eaten anything.

NURSE   You know we do it every two days. It's on your chart.

HANNAH   But I'm not bound up, dammit.

NURSE   Well, that's thanks to this.   *(Wags enema bag.)*

HANNAH   My body's gonna forget how to shit on its own if you keep shoving that tube up me. Leave me alone.

NURSE   Hannah, we don't want to have to restrain you.

HANNAH   Don't even try it.

NURSE   I'll get a sheet and tie you to the toilet if I have to, Hannah.

HANNAH   I have my mind! I know what I need.

NURSE   Doctor knows what's best for you.

HANNAH I haven't seen that little asshole in three months. How does he know what I need?

NURSE Look. I don't make a fortune doing this. I got enough on my plate without having to argue with you. I don't have the time.

HANNAH Make the time, dammit. There's more to taking care of people than reaming them out every other day. Don't I have any rights?

NURSE No.

Scene 2

(Hannah, played by the same actress, is now a young woman speaking a letter to Rachel.)

HANNAH Jesus, I love to fly. Rachel, it's the only way to see a place like Alaska. There's endless beauty up here, but some days it's almost too much. Rachel, I want beauty I can hold. *(Pause for her meaning to sink in.)* I miss you. Did you get the money I sent? Oh how I wish you could see the bald eagles. They're just like everything else up here—bigger than you could ever imagine. Mountains taller than a skyscraper. But you wouldn't know about that. My little home body. You've never seen a big city skyscraper. Hell, you've never seen a city. And they're quite the places to see but no place to live. Give me Alaska where the mountains grow like wildflowers. It'd be heaven on earth if you were here. Rachel, what's so wrong with wanting a little change? With wanting to see the world? *(As if listening.)* No, I can't be satisfied. Same old streets, same lake, same trees coloring up in the fall. You like that, knowing what you're going to see every day of your life. And it is pretty. But I can't spend my life looking out just one window. There's too much in the world to see. *(Pause.)* But my God, mountains and eagles and Broadway marquees, what's any of that when I hold it up next to you? *(Briefer pause.)* Well, I gotta sign off. This is gonna cost me an arm and a leg in postage as it is. *(Brief pause.)* I wish you'd write. It's been a while. Rachel, do you miss me at all? *(Pause, as if listening and hearing no answer.)* I'm not writing you again until I get some word from you. Just a penny postcard. Something. I'll still send money, but don't expect a letter. *(Brief pause.)* Don't stay mad. Please. I had to leave. Sneaking by Mr. Johnson's dog once or twice a week to see you like I'm some criminal wouldn't agree with me. Of course, Not seeing you Really doesn't agree with me. Should I come back? Or are you comfortable trying to be everything people think you are? You know what it comes down to; I just didn't mean enough. So here I am in Alaska and I've got to find more postage and a bigger envelope. I love you, Rachel. I truly do, and I wish you well. Think of me sometimes. Your old friend, Hannah Free.

(Greta's voice, breaking into a dream.)

GRETA You must have overslept. . . . Hannah . . . Hannah, wake up. *(During Greta's lines, Hannah slips into bed and wakes. Lighting changes to indicate change of consciousness. Greta leans over the bed.)* It's time to go see Gray—to go see Rachel. I checked her room. The coast is clear. Let me get your slippers and your wheelchair. Do you need to go to the bathroom?

HANNAH I'm sorry. Yes I do.

GRETA Oh, I always have to go when I get up. Do you use a bedpan, or can you use the toilet if I help you?

(Young Rachel appears.)

RACHEL Don't you let her go in that bathroom with you.

HANNAH *(To Rachel.)* Get a grip on yourself.

GRETA Here. Take a good grip on me; I'll help you up.

HANNAH I can't believe I'm finally gonna get to see her.

RACHEL Don't wake me. I'm sleeping soundly.

HANNAH We'll be quiet.

GRETA What?

HANNAH *(Legs over the side of the bed, concentrating on her feet as Greta slips on her slippers.)* Ghost.

GRETA Oh.

RACHEL Don't you call me a ghost.

(Brief pause, slight inclination of the head.)   Down the hall?
Don't look, too close. That's not me anymore.

HANNAH   These aren't my slippers.

GRETA   I bought you a new pair.

HANNAH   Are you adopting me?

GRETA   Maybe.

HANNAH   You Are hard up.

GRETA   Lean on me.

HANNAH   Just move the chair closer. I can get into it.

RACHEL   You're always so damn independent.

GRETA   Are you always so damn independent?

HANNAH   Move that chair closer.

(Greta and Hannah maneuver Hannah into the wheelchair.)

HANNAH   I appreciate this.

GRETA   I know.

Scene 3

(Rachel's room. Rachel is a form in the bed, her slender body hidden under blankets, a few tubes and cords attaching her to life. Hannah and Greta enter, Greta checking over her shoulder and closing the door softly.)

GRETA   The nurse has her Walkman on. Nights must get so long up here. *(Shushing herself.)* I'm sorry. Here, let me roll you over there. Then I'll just sit back here out of the way.

(Greta rolls Hannah to the bed. Greta takes a long look at Rachel, then moves away.)

HANNAH   Look at all this machinery. You could run a farm on all this electricity, all these goddamn tubes. You poor kid. *(Hannah slowly, tentatively, tenderly reaches out to touch Rachel's hair, her face, stroke Rachel's forearm with her fingertips.)* Go ahead and sleep, Rachel. I just wanna be here.

(Silence.)

HANNAH   You know, we were together on and off all our lives, but we were middle-aged—hell, we were Old—when we really fell in love. That's when you finally figure out what's really important. And that you may never get another chance at it. I stopped leaving, and she started letting me stay to breakfast. Her mother lived with her by then, and God that old lady hated me. She'd go without syrup rather than ask me to pass it. But nobody else wanted her. All she ever got from those other kids was Christmas cards. That old lady knew we did something Ungodly together, but she couldn't imagine what. Women who spend their lives with men just have no conception of pleasure.

(Silence.)

HANNAH   *(To Greta.)*   I guess I'm talking to you 'cause she's already heard everything I've got to say a dozen times. I just hope she's not too tired of me. We've got a burial plot together. Who knows if Marge'll put her there. The only thing in our favor is how cheap her kids are. I'm laying odds they're too cheap to fork over for another plot.

(The form stirs ever so slightly.)

HANNAH   She never wanted me to talk bad about 'em.
Motherhood. Glad I never did it. You know what I'd really
like is to have my carcass dropped in the woods somewhere. I
ate my share of wild game; it oughta be their turn. *(To
Rachel's still form.)*   I know. You want us both to have our pine
boxes and a proper burial. All right, Rachel. All those years
wandering, I did finally learn one thing. I learned where my
home is. *(She holds one of Rachel's hands in both of hers.)*

(The door opens. The nurse stands there.)

NURSE   Hannah? Hannah, you're in the wrong room.

HANNAH   Says who? *(Squints, looks closer.)*   Jesus, don't you ever
go home?

NURSE   A couple of the girls are out sick, so they're short. And I
got trailer payments to make. Look, Hannah, you should be
asleep. You're gonna make yourself sick. *(She hasn't noticed
Greta.)*   How in the world did you get yourself in here?
Hannah, you know how her family feels.

HANNAH   I'm her family.

NURSE   Let's take you back to your room.

HANNAH   What does it hurt? Rachel shouldn't be here alone, not
now, not right before dawn. Haven't you ever heard that's the
soul's midnight? That's when us old people die.

NURSE   Trust me, Hannah. People die all day long.

HANNAH   Please let me stay.

NURSE   Can't. I'm sorry, Hannah, but you're not supposed to be
here. Let's wheel you back to your room.

HANNAH   No!

NURSE   *(Getting angry.)*   Hannah, you're not the only person in this
Home. I've gotta get back to the desk. You come with me.

GRETA   *(After staying out of it, respecting Hannah's right to fight her own
battles, she finally speaks up.)*   I'm—Nurse, this is my great
grandmother's room. I brought Hannah to see her. I take full
responsibility.

NURSE   I haven't seen you before.

GRETA   I just flew in day before yesterday from Minnesota. Now look. This is Great Grandma Rachel's best friend. Of course, she should be here. Why don't you go back to your desk?

NURSE   Well, maybe for another fifteen minutes. Then you take her back to her room. I don't want to find her in here when I check again at three forty-five.

GRETA   I'll take her back to her room at dawn. She's not hurting anybody.

(Standoff.)

NURSE   Oh, all right. I guess she's not. But if that daughter of hers comes before Hannah's gone, I didn't see either one of you.

GRETA   Deal.

(Nurse exits.)

HANNAH   What a loada bull. I think I'm rubbin' off on you.

GRETA   Maybe you are. I hope so.

HANNAH   You hear that, Rachel? I get to stay.

Scene 4

(Greta is talking with Old Man.)

OLD MAN   Yes sir, I was in the CCCs. Planted trees. Rows and rows of trees. Lotta discipline, just like bein' in the military. Good preparation for WW Two.   *(Says the letters "WW.")*

GRETA   What did you do when the war ended?

OLD MAN   What d'ya mean "ended"?

GRETA   Oh.

OLD MAN   Say, aren't you Betty Grable?

(Marge enters. Greta and Marge see each other.)

MARGE   Greta?

GRETA   Yup.

MARGE   I had no idea you were in town.

GRETA   Nope.

MARGE   Weren't you even going to stop by?

GRETA   I wasn't planning to.

OLD MAN   *(To Marge.)*   Who are you? You a frienda Betty's?

MARGE   *(To Greta.)*   Betty?

GRETA   Betty Grable.   *(To Old Man.)*   Sir, I would like you to meet Tallulah Bankhead.

MARGE   I suppose that's an insult.

GRETA   Oh, I don't know.

OLD MAN   What kind of a name is Tallulah?

MARGE   Greta, what are you doing up here?

GRETA   Same thing you are. Visiting.

MARGE   That's nice of you. I guess. If you won't visit Me, at least you're spending time with Mom.

GRETA   *(To Old Man.)*   Thanks for talking to me.

OLD MAN   Have you seen my horses?

MARGE   Who me? Why no.

GRETA   Why don't you check down the hall?   *(Points.)*

OLD MAN   Much obliged.   *(Winks.)*   Save me a dance.   *(He exits.)*

MARGE   Are you staying in town long?

GRETA   As long as I want.

MARGE   Greta, must you be so rude?

GRETA   Yes, I think I must.   *(She turns to leave.)*

MARGE   If you could just stop being bitter for a little while, we could—Well, we could have lunch. We could talk about it.

GRETA   What's to say?

MARGE   So you're happy just to leave it like this? Blaming me for everything that's wrong in the world? Greta, I'm sorry. I made a mistake. Are you going to hold a grudge forever?

GRETA   Probably.

MARGE   Well, I'm sorry to hear that. Greta, I wish I could do it over. The door would be open.

GRETA   I hope so.

MARGE   Please come to lunch some day.

GRETA   I'll think about it. Maybe I'll even bring my lover. She likes a good lunch.

MARGE   Is this some kind of test?

GRETA   It's just the truth.

MARGE   Why am I not surprised?

GRETA   Yeah, why Aren't you surprised? You just knew I was gonna turn out "bad," huh?

MARGE   I didn't say that. *(After an uncomfortable pause.)* I guess I better go. I like to make sure they turn Mom often enough.

GRETA   Uh, Marge?

MARGE   Yes?

GRETA   What you did to my mom—

MARGE   Greta—

GRETA   Make sure you're not doing it again with Rachel, huh?

MARGE   I don't know what you mean

GRETA   I bet you don't. It's sad. Really sad. *(She exits.)*

MARGE   This isn't the same thing. This isn't the same thing at all.

Scene 5

(A memory. Rachel and Hannah, played by the same actresses, as girls.)

RACHEL   We better not.

HANNAH   *(Kisses her quickly.)*   There.

RACHEL   You stop that, Hannah.

HANNAH   You liked it.

RACHEL   I did not.

HANNAH   *(Kisses her quickly again.)*   You liked That one.

RACHEL   *(Wiping away the kiss with her hand.)*   Don't Do that.

HANNAH   Don't wipe away my kiss. Geesh. You wamme to go get Dewey Russell? You wanna kiss him?

RACHEL   Of course not. Don't be mean. I don't want to kiss anybody.

HANNAH   You mean it's not just me?

RACHEL   Well, especially not you.

HANNAH   Rachel!

RACHEL   Don't act so innocent. You know it's not right. If you don't feel funny about it, why are we in this chicken coop? Why aren't we on the front porch of your parents' house?

HANNAH   I'm shy.

(Rachel hoots.)

HANNAH   Don't laugh at me.

RACHEL   Hannah—

HANNAH   A lot of people laugh at me. Remember when Mrs. White tried to teach us all embroidery and I got all tangled up? And the other girls laughed and laughed at me, and Mrs. White tried not to? Not that I wanted to do something stupid like embroider anyway. I just didn't like being laughed at. So please don't laugh at me.

RACHEL   *(After a brief pause.)*   Hannah Banana, I wasn't laughing at you. It's just you make me nervous. You look at me like—like you're looking at me now. Like you're going kiss me again.

HANNAH   Want me to?

RACHEL   No.   *(Pause.)*   Yes.

(Hannah kisses her. It's a little longer kiss, though still quite innocent.)

RACHEL   Oh my.

HANNAH   You liked it?

RACHEL   Yes. Oh, why aren't you a boy?

HANNAH   Would you really want me to be a boy?

RACHEL   *(After a brief pause.)*   No.

HANNAH   You kiss Me this time.

RACHEL   *(Almost . . . but she just can't. Not yet.)*   I've got to go. I have chores to do.

HANNAH   Meet me here Saturday.

RACHEL   We're going into town for supplies.

HANNAH   How about Sunday after church?

RACHEL   I can't do this on a Sunday!

HANNAH   I got this idea I wanna try.

RACHEL   No no no. Whatever it is, no.

HANNAH   Monday. After school.

(Brief pause.)

RACHEL   All right. But just for a kiss.   *(She exits on the run.)*

HANNAH   *(Belts out her own version of "Bicycle Built For Two.")*   Rachel, Rachel, give me your answer do. I'm half crazy all for the love of you.   *(Singing fades as the Memory fades, and Hannah returns to her room at the nursing home.)*

Scene 6

(Hannah's room. Hannah is drowsing in her wheelchair, dreaming the previous scene. The mail lady enters, singing to herself, the proverbial bull in a china shop. She bumps into Hannah's chair.)

MAIL LADY   Oops. Sorry sorry. More mail. My you are popular. *(Handing Hannah one letter.)*   You get more mail than the rest of this place put together.

HANNAH   That's pretty damn sad.   *(Tears open envelope.)*

MAIL LADY   Hallmark?

HANNAH   That's for me to know.

MAIL LADY   You look really tired today, Hannah. Couldn't sleep?

(No answer.)

MAIL LADY   If your eyes are tired, I can read that to you.

HANNAH   I can still read.   *(Reading silently to herself.)*

MAIL LADY   Do you need to buy any stamps?

HANNAH   Haven't got any money up here.

MAIL LADY   Oh, yes you do. A little friend of yours left twenty dollars with the desk so you could treat yourself to some little extras. Would you like me to get you a Pepsi from the machine in the lounge?

(Hannah slowly looks up at her, just looks at her, a penetrating stare.)

MAIL LADY   I guess not. Well, the offer stands. I'm sure I'll be back tomorrow. You're always getting something. Bye now. *(She exits.)*

HANNAH   *(To audience.)*   I suppose some of you are thinking she means well. Don't kid yourselves. Wars are started every other week by some asshole who "means well." *(With a dark look she goes back to reading her letter.)*

(Spirit Rachel enters.)

RACHEL   So who's that from?

HANNAH   A friend.

RACHEL   *(Catching a glimpse of the postmark.)*   New Mexico?

HANNAH   *(Still reading.)*   Yes, but don't get all agitated.

RACHEL   Look at me.

HANNAH   Just one minute . . . thirty seconds . . .

RACHEL   I'm going back to my room.   *(She turns to exit.)*

HANNAH   No wait.   *(Lays letter in her lap.)*   I'm paying attention.

RACHEL   Your mind's in New Mexico.

HANNAH   That was years ago. She's just an old friend now. After working at Los Alamos all those years, she prob'ly glows in the dark.

RACHEL   Don't tell me how that woman glows in the dark. I suppose when I'm gone, you'll start conjuring Her up for company. Does she still miss you?

HANNAH   She always closes with that, but she's being polite. Her life's full.

RACHEL   You like that about her.

HANNAH   Yes. But you shouldn't envy her. She was no match for you.

RACHEL   You always said she was witty.

HANNAH   So are you.

RACHEL   Why doesn't she visit you?

HANNAH   I'm sure she'd rather remember me the way I was. And I guess I would, too. I don't want to see me in her eyes.

RACHEL   Are you coming tonight?

HANNAH   I hope so.

RACHEL   That girl's bringing you?

HANNAH   That's the only way I can get there.

RACHEL   Why's she helping you like this?

HANNAH   Oh Rachel, I don't know. I'm just glad she is.

RACHEL   Speak of the devil.

(Greta appears in the doorway, then enters.)

GRETA   Hi.

HANNAH   I'm surprised you're out of bed.

GRETA   I'll have you know I've been up here roaming the halls for over an hour. I've been talking to that old guy who was in here looking for his horses. He was in the CCCs. He planted "rows and rows of trees."

HANNAH   Kiddo, you sure do know how to have a good time.

GRETA   Don't tease. So how are you?

HANNAH   Tired.

GRETA   Oh by the way, I left a little money at the front desk . . .

RACHEL   Now you've got them tipping you.

GRETA   I hope you don't mind. I know you can't keep money in your room or it might get stolen, but this way you can treat yourself to a little something if there's something you want.

RACHEL   She Is thoughtful.

HANNAH   Thanks, kid, but I don't want anything.

GRETA   Not even a stamp or a pair of shoelaces? A magazine?

HANNAH   Read? Tie a shoelace? Gal, just the thought of it makes me tired. I used to have so much energy I just squandered it. Now I can't even make it down the hall alone. All my parts are worn out. But *I'm* still here, my eyes, my mind. I like to think I've refined myself down to the essentials. *(Very brief pause.)* So how are You doin'?

GRETA   Great. We going on vacation again tonight?

HANNAH   You're willing?

GRETA   I asked.

HANNAH   Three o'clock?

GRETA I'll be here.

HANNAH Thank you.

GRETA That's all right.

HANNAH No, it's not. I wanna give you something, and I finally
thought of what you might like.

RACHEL Just keep your clothes on, Hannah.

HANNAH *(To Rachel.)* Shush. *(To Greta, she gestures at the bottom
drawer of a dresser.)* In there.

*(Greta hesitates, then walks over, pulls the drawer out. There are several
old notebooks in it. Greta gingerly lifts them out, touching them tenderly,
gently.)*

HANNAH My journals. The Depression's in there some place.

GRETA You really mean it? You'd let me read them? I could quote
from them?

HANNAH Somebody might as well get some good outa them.

GRETA I'll try to skip over the personal stuff.

HANNAH Hell, if you can read my writing, you're welcome to it. Go
ahead. You might learn something.

GRETA I bet I will.

RACHEL I bet she will.

GRETA I'll see you tonight. *(She shoots a finger at Hannah.)*

HANNAH *(Shoots back.)* It's a date.

(Greta exits.)

RACHEL *(Snorts, shoots a finger at Hannah.)* It's a date. Aren't You
the nursing home Romeo.

HANNAH She Is pretty cute. Something about the way she walks
reminds me of you. You had such a pretty butt.

RACHEL Is that why you couldn't keep your hands off it?

HANNAH You know being near death has really brought out your
racy side.

RACHEL   You old flirt. You never let Me read those.

HANNAH   You're In 'em.

RACHEL   I hope you were kind.

HANNAH   Not always . . . Only two of those are journals. One's a
novel I wrote when I was snowed in. Beat alcoholism.

RACHEL   Am I in that too?

HANNAH   I think you'd recognize yourself.

RACHEL   Why did you give them to her?

HANNAH   *(Thinks. Sincerely.)*   I guess I want to pass something on.
I want somebody to know I was here.

RACHEL   Well, I know.

HANNAH   I want somebody to know you were here too. The real
you, not the you smilin' at church bake sales. I want
somebody to know about us who's not afraid to admit what
"us" means. I want somebody to know I took you to bed and
loved you.

RACHEL   We know. That's what matters.

HANNAH   Well, what about posterity?

RACHEL   Posterity. Good Lord, what next?

(The Old Man walks in on his walker. He stops, just stares at Hannah.)

HANNAH   Well?

OLD MAN   Well what?

HANNAH   What're you doin' in here?

OLD MAN   Isn't this my room?

HANNAH   No. You old men are over in the next wing. Ask the
nurse. She'll tell you where you belong.

OLD MAN   I'm lost.

HANNAH   I'll say you're lost. Go ask the nurse. She'll take you to
your room.

OLD MAN   Do I know you?

(Hannah starts to give a sharp retort, stops herself, looks him over a little more closely.)

HANNAH   You Do look a little familiar to me. I wish I could see a picture of you when you were younger.

OLD MAN   What's your name? Who are you?

HANNAH   Would you like to take a guess?

OLD MAN   *(An explosive.)*   No!

HANNAH   Then tell me who You are.

OLD MAN   *(Brief pause; he's obviously thinking, pondering the question.)* How soon do you need to know?

(The nurse appears.)

NURSE   Here you are.   *(She takes hold of the old man's walker.)*   He never knows where his room is.

OLD MAN   *(To Hannah.)*   I know you.

HANNAH   Not anymore you don't.

(The nurse starts to guide him out.)

OLD MAN   Your friend she don't say much.

(The Old Man and the nurse exit. Hannah and Rachel look at each other, knowing the Old Man has seen Rachel too.)

RACHEL   You should take a nap. Your little friend will be waking you up before you know it.

HANNAH   I used to wake You up.

RACHEL   I'd wake up, and my nightgown would be unbuttoned.

HANNAH   And I'd be at your breast takin' a drink.

RACHEL   I hope That's not in those books you gave that girl.

HANNAH   I wonder if she's got a little girlfriend. I'd bet anything she's like us.

RACHEL   You and your radar.

HANNAH   I never could convince you we weren't the only ones. And you'll never think what we did was okay.

RACHEL   Don't be silly. Didn't we sit on my porch holding hands, watching the sunset? Maybe not when we were thirty, but when we were sixty.

HANNAH   By then people just thought we were cute old ladies.

RACHEL   No one has ever thought you were cute. Everyone in this town knows what you are, Hannah, so they know about me too. I sat there with you knowing full well I was hanging out my bed sheets, but it meant so much to you, I finally just let go of my privacy. And I did it staying right where I was. I never ran. I stayed home and let people, family, lifelong friends and neighbors, know just what I am. You show me somebody else in one of your magazines from California who does that. Buncha cowards. They say who they are, but they say it in San Francisco preaching to the choir. I stood my ground, lived my life, and I loved you. I loved you despite everything I was brought up to believe. So don't get on your soapbox with me. Don't tell me anything.

(Silence.)

HANNAH   I'm tired.

RACHEL   So am I.

HANNAH   I wish we could take a nap together.

RACHEL   I'll be there.

INTERMISSION

ACT II

Scene 1

(Hannah is in her wheelchair, head drooping in sleep. Lights rise on Rachel telling her own letter circa World War II.)

RACHEL   You keep after me to write you more than three sentences. It took me half an hour to find a pencil, but now here goes. The ground is frozen. We've had snow. The Canada geese are on the lake, taking a rest on their way south. I walk over and listen to them honk; feed them cracked corn when I can get it. Marge is too interested in boys anymore to go with me. The boy she likes is going in the Army as soon as he graduates. It's hard to believe there's a war on as I'm standing by the water watching those geese take flight, calling out to each other. I read where they mate for life. I miss you, Hannah. I wish you'd stay home, but at least this time I know you're doing war work; you're not just running away from me. New Mexico sounds beautiful, but I'd miss my mulberry tree out back and my lilac bushes hanging over the driveway. You've been having dinner with the same woman all the time. What's that mean, "dinner"? I thought you were going to war; instead you're going to dinner. Well, I'm not knitting you any more warm socks, even if you are in the service. You're down there "having dinner" while I'm up here alone, squirming in my sleep. Well, I know people read your mail, so I won't say any more. Just know that I don't appreciate having to take long walks in the cold while you're down there—eating. You should be knitting Me socks. At least this time you left to serve in the war. We can pretend it was patriotism and not just wanderlust. I listen to the songs on the radio and I think of us. Hannah, I don't know how many more times I can let you leave me. At least I'm busy. I'm working at the hardware store, bookkeeping. The man who used to do their bookkeeping is in Italy. And that little Price boy who used to deliver the newspaper? His mother just got word. I'm so thankful you're not overseas. I think of how I used to send you away, then stay up all night and pray. Now I pray for you to come back. Be careful in New Mexico. Watch out for snakes. Check your boots. Come home soon. Was this long enough? I've never written such a long letter. You know I love you, but I'll say it anyway.

(Lighting fades on Rachel as the present intrudes. A young minister, full of damnation and salvation, enters. She/He walks over to the sleeping Hannah, opens her/his Bible and begins to pray over Hannah. Rachel fades as Hannah awakens. She's been happy dreaming of Rachel. She is startled and disgusted to have to wake up to this. The minister intones the 100th Psalm.)

MINISTER   ... Know ye that the Lord he is God; it is He that hath made us, and not we ourselves; we are His people ...

HANNAH   Who in hell are you?!

MINISTER   *(Trying to finish her/his line of scripture despite Hannah.)* ... and the sheep of His pasture. Enter into his gates with thanksgiving ...

HANNAH   I said who the hell are you?

MINISTER   ... and into His courts with Praise.

HANNAH   You! You can't just waltz in here like this and start spouting over me.

MINISTER   Mary, I am here to help you.

HANNAH   Don't you call me Mary. My name's not Mary.

MINISTER   It says Mary H. Freed on your door, Mary.

HANNAH   I don't give a rat's ass what it says on my door.

MINISTER   Mary, profanity is not the language of the Lord. Don't you want salvation? Don't you want to sleep in the loving arms of Our Lord Jesus Christ?

HANNAH   No!

MINISTER   You don't mean that, Mary. We All want to spend Eternity at peace with Our Maker. We All want to find Jesus waiting for us at the end of that tunnel of light. Mary, ask Jesus Christ into your heart, and He'll be there.

HANNAH   My name is Hannah. Hannah Free. Nobody has Ever called me Mary, not even my own mother. She knew early on I was not Mary material. So stop callin' me that and go pray over some poor asshole who can't talk back.

MINISTER   I can see I haven't caught you on a very good day.

HANNAH   I don't Have good days anymore.

MINISTER   Knowing Jesus would lighten your burden. Believe me *(Quoting again from the 100th Psalm.)*   the Lord is Good; His mercy is Everlasting.

HANNAH   Has it ever occurred to you that I have a right to my own opinions when it comes to religion?

MINISTER   Belief in Our Lord Jesus Christ is not opinion, Mary. It is a living, breathing, day to day fact of incredible beauty.

HANNAH   So you're on the road to Heaven?

MINISTER   *(Big smile.)*   I have my mansion reserved.

HANNAH   And I'm goin' to Hell.

MINISTER   If you don't accept Jesus Christ as your personal savior.

HANNAH   You sure do paint a meanspirited picture of Jesus. You get a lotta pleasure outa picturin' people burnin' in the fiery furnace, don'tcha? Seems kinda sick to me. Don'tcha think you oughta leave Judgment up to God?

MINISTER   God speaks to me and through me, Mary.

HANNAH   Bullshit.

MINISTER   *(Gathering up her/his Bible, preparing to exit.)*   We'll pray together again soon.

HANNAH   Lookit, I don't Wanna pray with you. I got my own views. Can't you respect that?

MINISTER   Mary, you are an old woman. God may be calling your name very soon. Next time the friendly hand of Salvation reaches out to you, Mary, I'd grab it.

HANNAH   My name's not Mary.

MINISTER   What a friend we have in Jesus. Never forget that, Mary. Read your Bible. And have a nice day.   *(Exits.)*

HANNAH   *(Yells after minister.)*   You can Have your mansion! I'm gonna be just fine in Hell!   *(Not as loud; no longer aimed at the door.)*   I'm all practiced up. How can she (he) expect to save anybody if she (he) won't listen to 'em? I Hate that. Hate that about bein' old. Nobody listens. They act like I'm just flappin' my gums to work up a breeze.   *(Slight pause.)*   Rachel?   *(She waits a moment.)*   Rachel?

(Rachel doesn't come. A faint light glows over the bed of the invalid Rachel.)

HANNAH   Well, if you're not gonna come I better get a radio. Drown out all the crazy people in the hall. 'Course they prob'ly think I'm crazy too, talkin' my head off in here to nobody. *(Listens.)* Jesus God, somebody's got *The Newlywed Game* on. Lotta these people up here are just hangin' by a thread; snap that little thread and they'd be gone. So what the hell are they doin' spendin' their last minutes on earth watchin' that goddamn *Newlywed Game*? Not that they watch. The nurse points 'em at the screen and they just kinda gape. *(Listens.)* Bedpan. Full. You can tell because somebody's swearin'. Rachel? One last game of checkers? *(Nothing.)* I'll let you win. *(Listens. Nothing.)* It's never really quiet up here. I should ask Greta if she'll bring me a radio so at least I choose my own noise. You don't hear anything, do you, Rachel? You're barely here. You keep tryin' to leave us all behind, and they just won't let ya. Do you hear me, Rachel? Are you still there?

Scene 2

(The past/memory. Rachel has her babies in a bassinet. Hannah enters, looking hale from her years in Alaska.)

HANNAH   I guess I shoulda knocked.

RACHEL   Yes, you should have.

HANNAH   *(The babies.)* They yours?

RACHEL   Yes.

HANNAH   Still pissed at me for leaving?

RACHEL   Yes. Must you swear?

HANNAH   Yes.

RACHEL   You didn't write that you were coming.

HANNAH   Didn't wanna warn you.

RACHEL   Are you just visiting?

HANNAH I believe I'm back.

RACHEL When will you know?

HANNAH Depends. How long you gonna stay mad at me?

RACHEL What has that got to do with it?

HANNAH That's got everything to do with it.

RACHEL I appreciated the money you sent from Alaska.

HANNAH Forget it.

RACHEL I didn't want to take it. I shouldn't have. But my garden froze early.

HANNAH You don't have to explain, Rachel. In fact, I wish you wouldn't. I wasn't paying for anything. If you ask me upstairs, I don't want you mixed up about why.

RACHEL I haven't asked.

HANNAH Not yet.   .

RACHEL What if I don't ask?

HANNAH I bet you will.

RACHEL I'm a mother now.

HANNAH So? Maybe they can spare me a tit once in a while.

RACHEL Get out.

HANNAH Look I'm sorry.

RACHEL You Are sorry. You are one sorry horse's patoot.

HANNAH Rachel!

RACHEL You left Me, remember?

HANNAH You got married!

RACHEL I didn't know that would mean I'd lose you too.

HANNAH What if I'd stayed? What were we supposed to do? Forget how we felt and just trade recipes?

RACHEL I needed you, Hannah.

HANNAH   Don't need me, Rachel. Want me. Put those babies down
   for a nap.

RACHEL   Hannah, it's still light out.

HANNAH   Rachel, I haven't seen you in over three years. I wanna
   See you. Put those babies to bed.

RACHEL   It isn't right.

HANNAH   Why? Because Mr. Johnson went belly up in the lake
   like some dimestore goldfish?

RACHEL   *(Trying not to find it funny.)*   What a way to put it. Only you
   would put it like that.

HANNAH   It's right for us, Rachel. Tell me you don't want it.
   (Pause as Rachel doesn't say anything.)   Up in Alaska when
   they're lightin' dynamite somebody'll holler out, "Fire in the
   hole!" I think that kinda sums us up.

RACHEL   You're just terrible.

HANNAH   And the more you shake your head, the wilder you are
   under the sheets. Put those babies to bed.

RACHEL   If we start—IF we start—promise you won't leave.

HANNAH   Cute babies. They got names?

RACHEL   Promise.

HANNAH   Some day I want you to bake me some biscuits wearin'
   just that apron, nothing else.

RACHEL   Hannah, give me an approximation. How long will you
   stay?

HANNAH   I don't know. I don't wanna know. Rachel, I need life to
   surprise me.

RACHEL   I'll bake you those biscuits if you'll stay 'til spring.
   (They kiss.)

HANNAH   You bake me those biscuits, I'll stay through summer.
   (She is caressing Rachel, kissing her between words.)   Maybe
   even 'til fall. You can carve me up for Halloween.   *(They kiss.)*
   But I promise, even if I go, I'll always be back.   *(Kisses her.)*
   I love you, Rachel. I gotta show you. Let me show you.

RACHEL   Let's put the babies to bed, then go upstairs. And take off your boots.

HANNAH   Can I leave my socks on?

RACHEL   If they're clean.

(They exit with babies.)

Scene 3

(Rachel's room. Rachel, just a figure in the bed, says nothing. Marge sits nearby, reading Good Housekeeping. She puts it down to stand up, stretch, and check on Rachel.)

MARGE   I guess I should go home soon, Mama. You know how Mason has to eat on time. When I started coming up here every day, he said it was my business; all he cared about was that I got home in time to cook his supper. So I do. Faithfully. Sometimes I cheat and mix it up ahead, then heat it up in the microwave. He doesn't care as long as when he sits down at exactly five thirty and leans forward with his fork there's something to stick it into. *(Brief pause.)* Oh dear, that sounded a little racy. And you know one thing Mason isn't is racy. The only time he gets romantic is after the Super Bowl.

(Pause as Marge looks at her mother, reluctant to leave, wishing for some word, some sign, some flicker of the eyelids; trying to think of things to say to her after so many months of one-sided conversations.)

MARGE   Did I tell you I talked to my brother? He says he can't fly home just now to see you. His youngest is still in drug rehab and Linda's on her third divorce, so Roy does have his troubles. I'm so grateful none of my family is into that dope. Not that I know of anyway. Who knows about Barbara's girl. I know, you told me, you warned me not to let how I felt about that draft dodger husband of hers get between us. I'll just never understand how anyone with your good sense could spend your life with that darn Hannah. Or without her. Did you get more love from her letters than I get from Mason snoring in front of the TV? Oh, Mama, I'll never understand. It's wrong. The Bible says so. Everybody I know says so. Not that I ever admit you did what everybody in this whole town knows you did. If somebody baits me, I just say how weird

Hannah was, but you were kind enough to stay friends with her. Not that you two didn't have your knock-down, drag-out fights. I'd hear you through the heating vent. But you and her both would rather lose an arm than say a word against each other in public. I should be like that about Mason. It's not his fault he needs a lot of sleep. At least he doesn't bore me with a lot of talk. But then he doesn't really listen either. Did Hannah listen to you? I guess she did finally. She stopped travelling and stayed home. I'll just never understand. You'd look at her like she could cure cancer. And now she wants to see you. She still won't leave you alone. I want you to die in peace. Hannah never brought you peace.

(The young Rachel is revealed standing nearby.)

RACHEL   She brought me something better.

MARGE   *(Can't see or hear this Rachel. Checks her watch.)*   Oh oh, I've really got to go. Mason'll be eating the placemat when I get home. Cutting it up in neat little squares. Goodnight, Mama. Sleep tight. I'll see you tomorrow. I'll see you.

Scene 4

(A memory of Hannah and Rachel in late middle age. Hannah is in bed. Rachel is at the sewing machine in her robe and hairnet, lining up a shirt to mend.)

HANNAH   Ra-chel.

RACHEL   *(Not taking her eyes from the cloth.)*   I need to finish this.

HANNAH   It can wait.

RACHEL   I thought this was your favorite shirt. I thought you Had to have it to wear to your cousin's funeral tomorrow.

HANNAH   I'll wear it like it is.

RACHEL   You will not.

HANNAH   He won't notice.

RACHEL   You're terrible.

HANNAH   Not as terrible as I'd like to be. Come to bed, Rachel.

RACHEL   This won't take five minutes. You can wait.

HANNAH   Since when?

(They eye each other.)

HANNAH   Please, Rachel, I wanna see my moonflower.

RACHEL   You're impossible.   *(But she does stand.)*

HANNAH   Leave the light on.

(There's a brief pause, a hesitation, but Rachel doesn't turn the light out. She sits on the edge of the bed. Hannah reaches up to touch Rachel's cheek, a lingering touch.)

HANNAH   I'll never get over this.

RACHEL   Oh Lord, you're going to talk me to death, aren't you?

(Hannah's hand pulls Rachel's head down for a gentle kiss. After the kiss, Hannah leans back, smiles and, in an echo from their childhood, says. . .)

HANNAH   Now you kiss Me.

RACHEL   Do you want my teeth in or out?

HANNAH   Rachel!

RACHEL   Hannah. Be quiet.   *(And this time she Does kiss Hannah, a long, light-fading kiss.)*

Scene 5

(Past fades into present. A couple of weeks later. Hannah is writing a letter to her one-time lover in New Mexico.)

HANNAH   Dear Jackie, you write such lively letters I can't compete. We don't do much white water rafting up to the Home. Yes, I think about New Mexico. But that's not where my life is. My life's here. I guess it always was. Go watch the sun rise over the desert for me, will ya? Good luck with your golf. Yours truly.

(Brief pause as she looks about to make sure Rachel isn't listening.) Much love, Hannah.

(Greta enters. Hannah doesn't notice her until she speaks.

GRETA Hi.

HANNAH Hi.

GRETA Feeling down?

HANNAH I don't know what you're doin' up here, week after week. If I was your age, kid, I sure as hell wouldn't be wastin' my time listenin' to some old babe beat her chops.

GRETA Well, you weren't as sensitive as I am.

(Hannah laughs.)

GRETA Hannah?

HANNAH Still here.

GRETA I hope you won't be mad.

GRETA Don't worry. Whatever it is, you can outrun me easy.

GRETA You know those books you loaned me?

HANNAH So what happened to 'em? Your dog eat 'em?

GRETA Hannah, they're wonderful. Especially the novel. I couldn't put it down.

HANNAH What's so bad about that?

GRETA You said the novel wasn't any good.

HANNAH That's what I was told.

GRETA I hope you don't mind. I xeroxed it and sent it to my—this professor friend of mine. Robin's an editor at one of the better women's presses, and I know I should have asked—

HANNAH But you thought I'd say no.

GRETA And I should have given you that chance. But Hannah, they want to publish it. I mean, it's not like it's some big publisher in New York. But people will read your book.

HANNAH Jesus, that's great. I'd love to see that. But you better tell 'em not to take too long at the printers.

GRETA Hannah! *(Makes a face.)* Why didn't it get published years ago?

HANNAH Hell, I tried. I sent it out. And I got it back. A lot. Some guy at Random House or Scribners, one of those, sent me a real snotty letter. Said he was "saving" me from "further embarrassment."

GRETA Why? Just because your book doesn't have men jacking off in some bullring in Spain?

HANNAH He claimed it was bad writing, but I s'pose the real problem was it's got two women together and neither one of 'em dies at the end. We didn't get to have happy endings in the Thirties.

GRETA But it's good. Didn't that count? How could he do that to you?

HANNAH Honey, people do that all the time. Critics ruin a career and then go to lunch. What the hell. I did what I wanted to in my life. Pretty much.

GRETA Except now.

HANNAH Well, even now—if I could be with Rachel—it's not so bad coming to the end if you're not alone.

GRETA *(Starts to cry; turns away.)* Shit.

HANNAH Don't blubber about it.

GRETA *(Has to laugh.)* You're awful.

HANNAH So why do you keep coming back?

GRETA The truth?

HANNAH Always.

GRETA She really is my great grandmother.

HANNAH She who?

GRETA Rachel. I wasn't lying when I told the nurse that.

HANNAH You're kiddin'.

GRETA   No, I'm not.

HANNAH   I met all her family.

GRETA   And you met me. Years ago. I was seven. You took me fishing so I couldn't hear Marge and Mom fighting about Daddy. We never came back after that. But I always remembered Rachel's hot chocolate. And going fishing with you.

HANNAH   *(Has remembered.)*   You wore that frilly little pink dress.

GRETA   Well, I don't anymore.

HANNAH   I never woulda had you figured.

GRETA   But I had You figured.

HANNAH   How long you been out?

GRETA   Officially? A couple of years. But I've always known who I had crushes on.

HANNAH   So you think I'm your lesbian heritage? You gonna write a song about me and sing it in some lesbo coffeehouse?

GRETA   I just wanted to know you better. You and Great Grandma.

HANNAH   Jesus Christ, this means Marge is your grandmother.

GRETA   Sorry. That's why I wanted you to get to like me before I told you.

HANNAH   Your parents were the ones who died in that car accident.

GRETA   Eventually. Mom was kind of like that.   *(Indicates Rachel's room.)*   I had power of attorney, and her living will put me in charge if Daddy died first, so it was up to me. I had to make a decision about the equipment.   *(Brief pause.)*   I let her go.

HANNAH   I wish I could do that for Rachel.

GRETA   Well, why don't you? What could they do to you? Arrest you? Lock you up somewhere?   *(She look around at the cell-like room in the nursing home.)*

HANNAH   Kiddo, you sure got a point. It'd be a damned shame if I had to spend the rest of my life locked up somewhere.

GRETA   You must just hate seeing her like that.

HANNAH But I don't know if I've got the guts to say the last goodbye.

Scene 6

(A scene from Rachel and Hannah's past.)

RACHEL What are you doing with that suitcase?

HANNAH Suitcase? What suitcase?

RACHEL The one under the bed. You just shoved it under there when you heard me coming. Where do you think you're going?

HANNAH The Himalayas.

RACHEL Why?

HANNAH I just need a change. Michigan's got no mountains.

RACHEL No, but it does have me.

HANNAH You could come.

RACHEL Hannah, I'm sixty-two years old.

HANNAH And you've never crossed the state line.

RACHEL I've never needed to. What are you looking for?

HANNAH I don't know, not exactly. New sights. Something different?

RACHEL Different just for the sake of different?

HANNAH Yes.

RACHEL Well, that's the stupidest thing I've ever heard in my life, and I've been listening to you for over fifty years.

HANNAH I'll be back.

RACHEL *(Suddenly very angry; years of anger.)* Don't you dare!

HANNAH What?

RACHEL   If you walk out that door, don't come back. Get your junk out of my garage. Don't send me a Christmas card. Just go. Go! Have a great time. But don't come back.

HANNAH   Jesus.

RACHEL   Don't' you know where your home is? Don't you know that yet? Hannah, a dog is smarter than you. What do I have to do? What do I have to say?

HANNAH   But what about what I want?

RACHEL   All our lives have been about what you want. This is about what *I* want. You've had your chance to roam. Now dammit, stay home! Stay with me. Sit on my porch with me and mow my lawn. Live with me, keep your clothes in my closet, clean my cat box. Don't just visit; be with me.

HANNAH   I know every inch of this place. Every flower, every nail, every bullfrog. There'll never be anything new to see.

RACHEL   Stay. If you can't find yourself, know yourself, Be yourself here with me, where can you?

HANNAH   Rachel . . .

RACHEL   It's not out there. It's here.

(Brief pause.)

HANNAH   I'll try.

RACHEL   You do better than try.

Scene 7

(Rachel's room at the nursing home in the late night/early morning. Hannah is sitting beside Rachel's bed. Greta sits nearby. Spirit Rachel is observing.)

RACHEL   Do it. Just do it.

HANNAH   Don't rush me.

GRETA   What?

HANNAH   I'm still not doing things quite the way she wants.

GRETA *(Sneaks a peek at her watch.)* It's almost dawn, Hannah.

HANNAH Just a couple more minutes. Let me sit with her just a couple more minutes.

GRETA Well, sure. Look, we don't even have to do it tonight. We can wait 'til tomorrow.

HANNAH I never believed in doing that.

RACHEL It's time.

HANNAH Rachel, what am I gonna do without you?

RACHEL You'll never be without me.

GRETA I look at the two of you, and that's what I want. My parents had that. I want to be with somebody for decades. I want to be comfortable and excited all at the same time. I want to say what I really think and trust her to still love me anyway. When my parents died, I didn't know what to do, because they were the people in my life who would always love me no matter what. But now there's Robin. And you. I've got family again.

HANNAH I'm just sorry you never really got to know Rachel.

GRETA But I do. Through you.

RACHEL Goodbye, kiddo.

GRETA Shit. I heard that. Oh, shit.

HANNAH So it's finally your turn to leave Me, huh, Rachel? *(Pause. Just the quiet.)* You didn't tell me she *(Greta.)* was family. In more ways than one. Isn't it too bad we couldn't have had Greta and her gal over to eat some potato salad on the porch? Wouldn't we of liked that? Finally somebody to talk to. We coulda visited Greta in Minneapolis—if I ever coulda got you outa town. Parades, festivals, gay newspapers, women's bookstores—gay and proud. Never in our wildest imaginings. I just wish it coulda come sooner. I wish you coulda seen it. *(Pause. Just the quiet. Finally, reaching for a cord/a plug.)* Is this the right one? I don't wanna just disconnect the clock. *(To Rachel's spirit.)* Are you sure this is what you want?

RACHEL Hannah, I've led a full life—my God, what a life—but it's over. Let it be over. Please, Hannah.

(Hannah's hand is on the plug. Marge enters.)

MARGE   What is going on here?

HANNAH   I'm giving your mother back her life.

MARGE   *(Grabs the wheelchair, pulls Hannah away.)*   Get away from her!

GRETA   Grandma, let go of her. Where do you get off?

MARGE   Greta?!

GRETA   Hannah's just doing what you should've done months ago.

MARGE   My God, did you wheel her in here? How could you?

GRETA   She's got a right to be here.

MARGE   She does Not.

GRETA   Of course she does. They're lovers.

MARGE   I hate that word.

GRETA   I don't give a shit. That's what they are.

MARGE   You shut up.

GRETA   *You* shut up.

MARGE   You don't know anything about this.

GRETA   Of course I do.

HANNAH   Girls, stop it. Marge, I'm glad you came.

MARGE   I'll just bet.

RACHEL   *(Quietly.)*   It's time.

HANNAH   It's time, Marge. You and I oughta do this together.

(Marge looks at Hannah, then down at Rachel.)

HANNAH   This isn't about you; it isn't about me. It's about her. We both love her—in our own ways. Saying goodbye to her hurts us more than anyone else on earth. But it's time.

(Silence.)

MARGE   I can't.

HANNAH   She's in pain, Marge. She's ready to go; we gotta let her go.

MARGE   I love her so much. And I've always been so jealous of you. Of how much you mean to her.

HANNAH   And I always resented you 'n that ugly little brother of yours. I wanted her to myself, but you two were always there.

MARGE   Did you always hate us?

HANNAH   I didn't hate you. In fact, I liked you okay when I could get a smile outa you. Once you grew up, forget it.

MARGE   Remember watching the moonflowers? We'd sit in the dark and watch those moonflowers open just like they were a fireworks display. They'd burst into bloom, but then in the morning they'd be gone. I still have some in my garden, but nobody appreciates them like we used to.

GRETA   I would.

RACHEL   Please.

MARGE   What was that?

HANNAH   *(Gestures at the still figure in the bed.)*   Her.

MARGE   That's not possible.

HANNAH   Listen.

RACHEL   Please.

MARGE   Please. She said please.

GRETA   She wants you to help her, Grandma.

HANNAH   *(To Marge.)*   How about you pull that one   *(Indicates a plug.)*   and I pull this one?   *(Points.)*   Greta, you turn off the IV. If anybody asks, if there's any trouble, I did it all. But I doubt they'll ask. It's time.

MARGE   *(To the bedridden Rachel.)*   Is this really what you want?

RACHEL   Let me go, Marge.

MARGE   I'll be so alone.

RACHEL   Get a dog.

MARGE   Mama!

HANNAH   That's my girl.

MARGE   I love you, Mama.

RACHEL   Do you love me enough?

MARGE   *(After a pause.)*   Yes.

HANNAH   After we disconnect all this, we'll sit with her 'til she's gone.

MARGE   Oh Mama.

HANNAH   *(Looks over at the spirit of Rachel.)*   Wait for me.

(Spirit of Rachel slowly reaches a hand toward Hannah, and Hannah is reaching toward her as the lights lower.)

CURTAIN

MOVIE QUEENS

Cast of Characters

Young Meg	Ramon
Young Adele	The Reporter
Meg	Stage Manager
Adele	Barry
Sydney	Roald
Vera	PseudoMeg I
Bonita	PseudoMeg II
Jilly	Elevator Operator
Loren Gerard	Fan
Mike	

Setting

1930s Hollywood; 1980s Broadway.

Notes

The author recommends that actors be double, triple, and quadruple cast. The play can be performed with a minimum of eight actors, or the maximum of nineteen.

Movie Queens premiered in Chicago on September 15, 1990 at the Zebra Crossing Theatre, directed by Marlene Zucarro. A one-act version of *Movie Queens* was first produced by Stonewall Repertory in New York City in 1986.

Summary

Movie Queens is a fantasy based in all those rumors of who Was or Wasn't in Hollywood. Adele Montrose and Meg Elliot are two old movie stars in rehearsal for a play in the 1980s. Their feud dating back to the 1930s is famous, but few know the real reason behind the animosity—Meg and Adele were lovers, a passionate affair that ended with an Oscar. *Movie Queens* flashes back and forth between the 1980s and the 1930s, exploring the price of celebrity with humor and passion.

Author's Note

I wrote this one purely for my own entertainment—it's the Hollywood we never got to see.

ACT I

Scene 1

(The action of the play will bounce back and forth between the early 1980s and the 1930s, New York City and Hollywood. We open with a catty 1980s TV gossip columnist.)

LOREN GERARD. *(Speaking into an imaginary camera.)* Liza, all I can say is remember your mother. Speaking of over the hill and over the rainbow, this reporter can hardly wait for the new Clyde Chamberlain play to open. Not that anyone is expecting anything of Clyde. It's Adele Montrose and Meg Elliot we'll be paying our thirty bucks a seat to see. What a casting coup. Two of the greatest movie queens of the silver screen, those art deco icons, the elusive Adele Montrose and the ever vibrant Meg Elliot, both in one play, under one roof. Will the gloves be on or off? New York can hardly wait.

Scene 2

(Still the 1980s. The stage of a theater. Rehearsal. The elder Meg Elliot is lounging in her chair. The director, Sydney, is pacing.)

MEG Sydney, stop pacing. She'll be here.

SYDNEY Two hours late. She is two hours late!

MEG Adele has always been late. It's part of her persona.

SYDNEY Do you think she overslept? Do you think she's dead?

MEG When Adele was sixteen—or eight, depending on which bio you believe—When Adele was young, just getting started in silents, someone told her that a star is never on time, and Adele's been late ever since.

SYDNEY Well, that little attitude will Not work in the Theater. It's Infuriating! I'm going to talk to her about it the minute she flounces in that door. If she ever does.

MEG Talk softly.

SYDNEY *(Trying to calm down.)* I suppose she is nervous. This is the first play she's done since . . . *(Falters.)*

MEG Kingdom come, thy will be done, on earth as it is in heaven.

SYDNEY You really don't like her, do you, Meg? I thought that whole feud business was just hype.

MEG Oh, don't be silly. I like Adele. I've always liked Adele. Hell, I'm positively wild about Adele. But that doesn't sell papers.

SYDNEY When I was kid, I used to watch her movies on the late, late show.

MEG If I were you, I wouldn't tell her that.

SYDNEY She had such incredible cheekbones.

MEG I imagine she still does.

SYDNEY But of course you were brilliant. I loved those musicals you were in.

MEG I did look darned cute dancing around in a bowl of fruit. I was the original fruit of the loom. Did you see that picture? Forty-two women dancing in a fruit bowl. I was, of course, the love interest, so I got to be the cherry. The bad girl was a banana.

SYDNEY Dammit, I wish she'd come.

MEG Now that's one thing Adele never had a problem with—or so I've heard.

SYDNEY Why aren't there any great stars like the two of you anymore?

MEG Dear, we haven't passed on.

SYDNEY You know what I mean.

MEG I suppose I do.

SYDNEY Hollywood was really something in those days.

MEG Yes, it was. *(Her mind is drifting back.)*

Scene 3

(The 1930s. The studio. Meg, wearing a dress made out of money, is talking on the phone.)

YOUNG MEG No, Mom, I haven't met any nice men yet . . . Yes, I Have met Clark Gable and believe me he isn't nice . . . You're right. I'm Not trying.

(Barry appears with clipboard; points to watch.)

YOUNG MEG Mom, I gotta go . . . Yes, I Know there's still time for me to get a teaching certificate, but I'm really doing great at this. Really.

BARRY Come on, Meg. Stardom awaits.

(Meg catches a glimpse of Adele crossing the stage, followed by someone writing furiously on a pad of paper, hanging on her every word.)

YOUNG MEG *(Staring after Adele, says to her mother over the phone.)* I love you, too. *(Hangs up.)* Isn't that Adele Montrose?

BARRY *(Taking her arm.)* She's on loan but not to you.

YOUNG MEG *(Still watching Adele as Barry leads her away.)* Clark Gable? No thank you.

Scene 4

(The 1980s. Rehearsal. Just a moment later.)

SYDNEY You don't think she forgot today was the first day of rehearsal, do you?

MEG She'll be here. A great actress knows how to build a great entrance.

(Time tilts and the young Adele sweeps on-stage, sweeping us once again into the 1930s of Meg's memory.)

MEG *(Looks at the woman.)* And Adele was always worth waiting for.

Scene 5

(Lights up on a party in the 1930s. This is Adele's scene, but the young Meg should stand at the edge of the stage, drink in hand, perhaps with Mike but obviously watching Adele and the scene. A young man in a tuxedo scurries up to Adele.)

ROALD   Adele. Miss Montrose. Wait for me. Wait! I'm supposed to be with you.

YOUNG ADELE   *(Ice.)*   Do I know you?

ROALD   I brought you here.

YOUNG ADELE   Oh, yes. My chauffeur.   *(Starts to walk away.)*

ROALD   *(Miffed.)*   I am not. You know perfectly well he told me to be your escort tonight. The blurb for Hedda's column is already arranged. So let's get over there and say hi to her.

YOUNG ADELE   *(Dripping venom.)*   Don't-you-dare talk to me that way. Is your name above the title? Can anyone even find your name in the credits? Bring me a drink; then get lost.

ROALD   Fine by me. Be that way. But He's going to hear about it.

(Adele turns away to examine a painting or her fingernails, whatever's handy, ignoring Roald as he glowers, exits. A woman approaches Adele.)

VERA   Hi, sweetie.

YOUNG ADELE   *(A frigidaire.)*   Hello.

VERA   *(Baby talk.)*   Is Adele still angry with Vera?

YOUNG ADELE   Angry? Who me angry? Vera, just because you and that Scandinavian spent two weeks in Tia Juana muff-diving you think I might be angry?

VERA   It's over.

YOUNG ADELE   I'll bet.

VERA   Who was the boy?

YOUNG ADELE   Oh, just another one of my fans.

VERA   Now if he were a woman I'd be worried.

YOUNG ADELE   Vera, go away.

(Roald reappears with champagne.)

ROALD   I hope pink champagne's all right. It's all they've got.

VERA   Don't worry. She Loves pink champagne.

YOUNG ADELE   It will do—what was your name again?

ROALD   Roald. Roald Alexander.

YOUNG ADELE   Born Harry Smith, I'll bet.

VERA   Lighten up, Adele. You were named after a street in Chicago.

YOUNG ADELE   Roald, be a dear and go play.

ROALD   *(Frowns.)*   Oh, all right. But we've got to say hi to Hedda soon or she's going to be miffed.

YOUNG ADELE   I don't give a goddamn what that bitch has to say.

ROALD   Well, I do.

VERA   *(Good-naturedly to Roald as he is turning to exit.)*   Oh so does she. Don't let her fool you. She'll be along.

(Roald gives her a nervous half smile in thanks, exits.)

YOUNG ADELE   You are so patronizing.

VERA   I think nice is the word you're looking for.

YOUNG ADELE   You'll always be supporting cast, Vera, playing "character" parts.

VERA   And I'll work steadily until the day I die.

(Adele drains her glass, looks away, trying to ignore her.)

VERA   Would it help if I said I was sorry? Sometimes I need to be with other women to realize just how much I want to be with you. More champagne?

YOUNG ADELE   No.

VERA   Remember the night you dipped my breasts in champagne?

YOUNG ADELE   *(Giving her a level gaze.)*   Vera, I have dipped dozens of breasts in champagne.

VERA   Then I melted chocolate and poured it down your belly.

YOUNG ADELE   Vera, go away before I make a scene.

VERA   You'd never dare.   *(Adele is furious, but it's true.)*

Scene 6

(The 1980s, rehearsal, even later. Meg is lost in thought and memory. Sydney is furious.)

SYDNEY   Three hours late. No one is three hours late for first rehearsal. For Any rehearsal. It just isn't done.

MEG   Calm down, Sydney, she'll be here. Adele always liked to cause a stir but never a scandal.

SYDNEY   Why aren't people ever what you dream they'll be? My God, Adele Montrose. I was elated when I signed a contract to direct Adele Montrose, and this is what happens.   *(Scornful.)*   Adele Montrose.

MEG   *(Sees the elder Adele at the back of the theater beginning her entrance.)*   That's right, honey. "The" Adele Montrose. In all her glory.

(Adele Enters. She and Meg eye each other.)

ADELE   Lovely outfit, darling.

MEG   *(Who is in jeans or sloppy pants, an old shirt or sweatshirt.)*   I think it's me.

ADELE   Yes. Unfortunately. So how do you like mine?

MEG   Very subtle.   *(It's not.)*   I'm not disappointed.

ADELE   What a nice change.

MEG   *(Pointed.)*   I was never disappointed in your wardrobe.

SYDNEY   *(Clearing throat.)*   Ahem.

ADELE   *(Still looking at Meg.)*   It's been a long time.

MEG   And my haven't they been good years?

SYDNEY   Ahem.

ADELE   Who's your little friend?

MEG   Oh, this is Sydney. Our director. Syd, this is Adele
Montrose. You remember. She was supposed to be here for
rehearsal—three hours ago.

ADELE   *(Turning on the charm, takes Sydney's hand.)*   Oh dear, am
I late?

SYDNEY   *(Melts.)*   Maybe a smidge, but it's no big deal. Really.

MEG   *(To Adele.)*   You've still got it.

ADELE   When I don't, I fully intend to shoot myself.

SYDNEY   *(Marveling.)*   You've still got those amazing cheekbones.

ADELE   *(To Meg.)*   Is this   *(Gestures at Sydney.)*   one of your
pranks?

(Sydney laughs, delighted.)

MEG   Sydney, could we possibly rehearse a page or two of this
play? You remember, we're supposed to be rehearsing a play?
It's almost lunchtime, and I am starving.

ADELE   You always did have a tremendous appetite.

MEG   I still do.

(Moment.)

SYDNEY   I suppose we Should start. Maybe we could just read
through the first scene together, how does that sound? Would
that be all right with both of you?

MEG   A bold and daring move, Sydney, but I think we can
handle it.   *(To Adele.)*   Can you sit in that thing?

ADELE   *(Taking her time, milking the moment, sits.)*   Yes, I can sit.

MEG   Dandy. Let's start.

ADELE   But where is the author? We aren't going to start without
Mr. Chamberlain, are we?

MEG   You really are late, Adele. Clyde finally started crying, so we sent him home.

ADELE   A star is never on time. He should know that.

MEG   These aren't the old days, Adele.

ADELE   *(A look of quiet fury.)*   I realize that.

SYDNEY   Page one? Let's just start at the very beginning.

ADELE   Novel approach.

MEG   Once upon a time, in a magic land called Hollywood . . .

SYDNEY   *(Begins leafing through her script.)*   What? Wait. I don't see that in my copy.

Scene 7

(The 1930s. The party. Meg is obviously looking for something or someone. Vera notices her.)

VERA   Dear, did you lose something?

YOUNG MEG   No. I'm just looking for someone.

VERA   Aren't we all?   *(Moves in closer.)*   Maybe I can help.

YOUNG MEG   I don't think so.

VERA   You'd be surprised.   *(Meg and Vera give each other a long look.)*

YOUNG MEG   Thanks for the thought, but I've got a specific item in mind.

VERA   Well, if you decide you'd rather do business with an established firm, my number's on every powder room wall in town.   *(And with a very sexual look, she walks away.)*

YOUNG MEG   *(Watching Vera's exit.)*   God, I'm glad I left Michigan.

Scene 8

(The 1980s. A few days into rehearsals. Meg is eating a sandwich. Adele is picking at a container of yogurt.)

ADELE You Still eat like a horse. It's simply amazing. I'd weigh four hundred pounds if I ate like that.

MEG You do your nails for exercise; I walk. Three miles every morning in Central Park, hoping someone will recognize me.

ADELE You don't fool me, dearie. You're just hoping you'll run into Garbo. You were always rather hoping you would "run into" Garbo.

MEG Oh, you know I never—seldom—sleep with actresses. Besides, Greta's an old, old *(Adele mouths two more olds.)* friend. She comes to my place in Maine to swim. She and Van Johnson. You don't see any of the old crew, do you?

ADELE All of the interesting people are dead.

MEG Thanks a lot. I thank you. Jimmy Stewart thanks you. Myrna Loy thanks you . . .

ADELE Oh, do be quiet.

MEG Here comes Sidney. I think she's with her drug dealer. *(Squints.)* Or is that one of the producers?

ADELE Meg?

MEG Hmm? Like a bite? *(Extends sandwich.)*

ADELE No. No, thank you. *(A moment of vulnerability.)* Meg, am I doing all right?

MEG You're doing fine. You just need to project more. You're not reaching the balcony at all.

ADELE I don't give a damn about the balcony. I only play to the orchestra seats.

MEG Brother.

ADELE *(Looking about.)* Some days I wonder why I ever left my island.

MEG Don't be such a damned hermit. You never used to be.

ADELE You just love all this, don't you?

MEG New York? The theater? This is where I always wanted to be.

ADELE I remember you always used to give that speech. Then you'd pass out.

MEG   All those years I spent in Hollywood churning out musicals and screwball comedies, not a day went by that I didn't wish I was here instead—on Broadway.

ADELE   I thought you seemed very content at times.

MEG   *(Moment.)* Hollywood did have its moments.

ADELE   I wanted to be a motion picture star more than anything else in the world.

MEG   So I found out.

ADELE   *(This is hard for her to ask, but she's been dying to know.)* Are you here—in New York—alone?

(Meg ignores the question, lights a small cigar.)

ADELE   I suppose Not, knowing you. I'm sure you've got some little thing hanging on your every word.

MEG   And you have your wolfhounds or iguanas or something.

ADELE   Well, I did have a husband, as you recall.

MEG   *(Dripping with remembered venom.)* Yes. *(Brightens.)* I was sorry to hear about his passing.

ADELE   I appreciated the flowers you sent for his funeral, though I believe horseshoe arrangements are more appropriate for the Kentucky Derby.

MEG   Well, it's the thought that counts.

ADELE   Exactly. *(After a pause.)* You know you never did answer my question. Are you . . . in a relationship?

(Pause.)

MEG   Not anymore. My lover got her consciousness raised and left to go homestead in Canada with three other women and four female cats. I believe they all sleep together. I couldn't compete.

ADELE   I find that hard to believe.

(Moment.)

MEG   I can't believe how many years it's been.

ADELE   Decades and decades since we first met at that dreadful party. Of course, I was an infant at the time.

MEG   Weren't you bored being married?

ADELE   Yes, but I was safe. I never felt a bit safe when I was with you.

MEG   You weren't. What is it? Have I got mustard on my chin? What are you looking at?

ADELE   You. It was a hard habit to break.

MEG   Ever wish you hadn't?

Scene 9

(The 1930s. That party. Meg is finally drunk enough to go after what she wants. Adele is sitting on a couch with Roald passed out in her lap; she is relentlessly drinking champagne, glass in hand, bottle at her elbow.)

YOUNG MEG   *(Approaches Adele.)*   Hi.

YOUNG ADELE   *(Affecting a deep, affected delivery.)*   Hello.

YOUNG MEG   He looks comfortable.

YOUNG ADELE   I hope so, because I'm not.

YOUNG MEG   Who is he?

YOUNG ADELE   Oh, I don't know. My date, I suppose.

YOUNG MEG   Mine fell in the pool.

YOUNG ADELE   Did he drown?

YOUNG MEG   For all I care.

YOUNG ADELE   *(A pause as she studies Meg with a bit more interest.)*   Weren't you on some magazine cover last week billed as "America's Sweetheart"?

YOUNG MEG   America's in deep trouble.

YOUNG ADELE   I think I'm going to stand up.

YOUNG MEG   Good luck.

(Adele struggles to free herself, but Roald just snuggles closer. Meg, moving with drunken care, rolls Roald off onto the floor. He doesn't wake up. Meg offers Adele a hand to pull her to her feet. Adele's hand remains in Meg's a moment longer than is strictly necessary.)

YOUNG ADELE   Thank you.

YOUNG MEG   My pleasure.

YOUNG ADELE   It's funny that we've never met before.

YOUNG MEG   It's a big town. And I don't go to many of these parties.

YOUNG ADELE   What kind of parties do you go to?

YOUNG MEG   Actually, I don't. I like to read, go horseback riding on the beach, that sort of thing.

YOUNG ADELE   Yet here you are at this Incredibly dreary party. Why?

YOUNG MEG   *(Brief pause.)*   I thought it might be interesting.

YOUNG ADELE   And why, pray tell, was this party supposed to be interesting? Did I miss something?

YOUNG MEG   Actually   *(Brief pause.)*   I'd heard you were going to be here, and I've been wanting to meet you.

YOUNG ADELE   Really?

YOUNG MEG   A friend told me you and I have something in common.

YOUNG ADELE   And what would that be?

YOUNG MEG   *(Hedging.)*   Well, we're both famous.

YOUNG ADELE   So is Helen Hayes. Why aren't you talking to her?

YOUNG MEG   Is she here?

YOUNG ADELE   I am very fond of cats. Are you fond of cats?

YOUNG MEG   My friend didn't mention cats. He said we have something else in common.

YOUNG ADELE   Who exactly is your friend?

YOUNG MEG   Ramon Riviera.

(Dawn solidly breaks. They are both now very sure of what they both are and what they both want.)

YOUNG ADELE   I hope you haven't made the mistake of falling in love with dear Ramon.

YOUNG MEG   You're very funny.

YOUNG ADELE   You haven't seen anything yet.

YOUNG MEG   That's quite true. But I would like to.

YOUNG ADELE   You have lovely hair. Is it real?

YOUNG MEG   Everything about me is real, Adele.

YOUNG ADELE   I prefer to judge that for myself.

YOUNG MEG   Would you care for a lift home?

YOUNG ADELE   I don't want to go home.

YOUNG MEG   Where do you want to go?

YOUNG ADELE   Wherever you're going. You don't live with your mother or anyone, do you?

YOUNG MEG   Nope. I have my very own apartment, just like a real grown-up person. Why? Don't you?

YOUNG ADELE   The maid spies for the studio. The last time I brought a woman home I nearly lost my contract.

YOUNG MEG   *(Moving in close.)*   You'll be safe with me.

YOUNG ADELE   Somehow I doubt that. Don't stand so close. Someone here may not be as comatose as we think.

YOUNG MEG   Well, come on then. What the hell are we waiting for?

(Adele and Meg exit.)

Scene 10

(Still in the 1930s. It's that same night/early morning. Adele and Meg enter Meg's apartment.)

YOUNG ADELE   *(Looking around.)*   So you're from the Midwest.

YOUNG MEG Michigan. How could you tell? Did the knotty pine give me away?

YOUNG ADELE Actually it's that lovely stuffed trout over the fireplace.

YOUNG MEG I'm so impressed you can recognize a trout when you see one. I guess you didn't grow up at the Plaza yourself.

YOUNG ADELE Only one bedroom?

YOUNG MEG I don't like company, unless they're very special company. *(Moving closer.)* Let me give you the grand tour.

YOUNG ADELE I must send Ramon flowers.

YOUNG MEG See how you like the tour first.

YOUNG ADELE I must warn you that I bite.

YOUNG MEG You're going to do a lot more than just bite.

YOUNG ADELE Take off your dress.

YOUNG MEG Here?

YOUNG ADELE *(Moving closer to undo the dress.)* Yes, here. Now. I can't wait.

YOUNG MEG You know you're just not what I expected.

YOUNG ADELE *(Biting Meg's bare shoulder.)* Disappointed? Did you want an ice goddess? *(She kisses Meg, her hands running down Meg's back to cup her buttocks. It's a deep, breathless kiss.)*

YOUNG MEG You're so lovely. Come to bed.

YOUNG ADELE *(Pauses for a moment.)* I have to leave before daylight.

YOUNG MEG Why? Are you a vampire? Besides *(Gestures at a window.)* you're too late. It's already light.

YOUNG ADELE *(Pulls the cord on the Venetian blind. Light streams in.)* Oh, God, I can't stay.

YOUNG MEG You're joking.

YOUNG ADELE No, I'm not. I can't. He checks. The maid . . .

YOUNG MEG Adele, you're not leaving.

YOUNG ADELE   Look, I'll call you.

YOUNG MEG   Go to hell.   *(She stoops to pick up her dress, though she doesn't bother putting it on.)*

YOUNG ADELE   He can't find out.

YOUNG MEG   Fine. Go. Jesus, don't let me keep you.   *(She turns; starts to walk away.)*

YOUNG ADELE   When can I call you?

YOUNG MEG   *(Looks over her shoulder.)*   Don't.

YOUNG ADELE   You mean it's now or never?

(Meg pauses, walks back to Adele and begins unzipping her dress. Adele opens her mouth to protest, but Meg closes it with a kiss. Adele's dress drops to the floor. Adele steps away, out of the dress.)

YOUNG ADELE   This is too much to ask.

YOUNG MEG   Adele, come to bed. I want breakfast in bed, and I want it to be you.

YOUNG ADELE   Please don't. I just can't. Please give me my dress.

YOUNG MEG   You'll be sorry.   *(She holds out a dress to Adele—the wrong dress, but Adele doesn't notice.)*

YOUNG ADELE   I already am.

YOUNG MEG   I think you should fire your maid.

YOUNG ADELE   Don't hang up when I call.

YOUNG MEG   It's daylight, Adele. Go on. Go on home to Mommy and Daddy. This is bullshit.   *(She starts to exit into bedroom.)*

YOUNG ADELE   *(Struggling to get into the dress.)*   How about dinner Saturday night? We could eat early . . .

YOUNG MEG   Forget it. I only sleep with adults.   *(She exits.)*

YOUNG ADELE   Be a sport.

(Silence.)

YOUNG ADELE   How long do you stay mad?

(Silence.)

YOUNG ADELE   *(Still struggling with the dress.)*   I want to stay, but you know I can't. I'm playing the Virgin Mary in this picture, so I have to be especially careful. Can't you understand?

(Silence.)

YOUNG ADELE   Let me come back?

(Silence.)

YOUNG ADELE   I will be back, do you hear me?

(Silence. She looks at the bedroom door one more moment.)

YOUNG ADELE   Dammit!   *(She exits.)*

Scene 11

(The 1980s. A little further into the rehearsal process. Sydney is trying to speak rationally.)

SYDNEY   Miss Montrose—Adele—

ADELE   Miss Montrose.

SYDNEY   There are no close-ups in the theater. You need to act with your entire body.

ADELE   I am.

SYDNEY   I'm afraid you're not.

ADELE   What exactly do you want me to do—shimmy?

(Meg laughs.)

SYDNEY   We open in ten days.

ADELE   I am well aware of when we open, and I do not intend to step onto this stage opening night and shimmy.

SYDNEY   *(Through gritted teeth.)*   I don't want you to shimmy. I just want you to stop acting from the neck up. Meg is so wonderful.

MEG   Oh, oh. We're in trouble now.

ADELE   I know Meg is wonderful. But I'm not Meg.

MEG   She let you off easy on that one, Sydney. Take my advice and shut up.

SYDNEY   *(To Adele.)*   Well, do the best you can.

ADELE   I am. Unfortunately it doesn't seem to be good enough. *(She rises, picks up her bag, exits.)*

SYDNEY   *(Calling after Adele.)*   You can't just   *(Brief pause; Adele's gone.)*   leave. How could she do that? She's impossible. Shit. Shit! Oh well. We can still do your scene at the courthouse.

MEG   *(Rising.)*   No, Sydney, "we" can't. "We" aren't doing anything without Adele. Dear, by tomorrow I suggest that you learn the fine art of diplomacy.   *(Meg exits.)*

SYDNEY   Not you, too!   *(Collapses, Pepto-Bismol in hand.)*   My God. Next time I'm going to direct a play with little children. And dogs!

Scene 12

(Still in the 1980s. Adele is in her hotel suite, looking in her mirror, drink at hand.)

ADELE   Not bad. Not great but not bad. Meg doesn't look a day over fifty. Of course, she Is younger. How much? Seven years? Six? Oh, who remembers. I always lied and she told the truth. Infuriating woman! God, I was such an idiot. Why didn't I just leave her that night and never come back? I never should have seen her without her dress. How could I resist?

Scene 13

(The 1930s. Meg is reading a card attached to a box of roses. She drops the box in a wastebasket already overflowing with rejected tokens—perhaps a lobster claw hangs over the edge. Meg walks away. Lights move to another part of the stage where Vera and Adele are at a restaurant, dining.)

VERA   *(Over her martini.)*   So. How long are you going to keep this up?

YOUNG ADELE   What?

VERA Pining. It really doesn't become you, dear. Women are supposed to grovel at Your feet.

YOUNG ADELE I'm Not grovelling. I've just sent her flowers. Roses. Just a few dozen. Orchids. Shrimp. Lobsters. Notes signed in blood.

VERA I wonder if you're kidding.

YOUNG ADELE She has the loveliest skin.

VERA Do you mind if I don't want to listen to this?

YOUNG ADELE Oh. Sorry.

VERA I know we both have our flings. And we've been known to tell each other the details when we're drunk, but this is one I don't think I want to hear about.

YOUNG ADELE But Meg and I didn't even do anything. A kiss. Nothing.

VERA Nothing, huh? Listen to you. Face it, Adele, this one's really gotten to you. You want in her jammies so bad you lie awake nights.

YOUNG ADELE *(Grumpy.)* Oh how do you know?

VERA If you're going to lie awake nights, you might as well be having fun. Come home with me.

(Brief pause.)

YOUNG ADELE I don't think so, Vera.

VERA My God, fidelity. And to a woman who won't even answer your phone calls. *(In her little girl voice.)* You'd rather dream about her than sleep with me.

YOUNG ADELE I don't mean to hurt you, Vera. But it's true. I can't stop thinking about her. It wouldn't be fair to make love to you when all I want—I'm sorry, darling. She's really gotten to me.

VERA And how? By teasing you.

YOUNG ADELE She isn't teasing.

VERA The next time I fall in love remind me to play a little hard to get.

YOUNG ADELE   I tell you she's not playing. She really is angry. I'm the one who walked out on her. It was daylight.

VERA   You are rather like sleeping with a vampire.

YOUNG ADELE   She said something to that effect. It was definitely not a point in my favor.

VERA   Oh, don't worry, Adele, she can't keep this up. She's crazy if she doesn't say yes.

YOUNG ADELE   I think we're all crazy.

VERA   Oh, don't get tiresome.

YOUNG ADELE   Why do we do this? It's not normal. It's—it's—

VERA   Just so much fun.

Scene 14

(Another scene from the past. Meg is judging a Meg Elliot look-alike contest. A "Meg Elliot" prances up. A few moments into the scene, Adele enters and watches, amazed. Meg doesn't see her at first; she's busy chatting with her breathy "look-alike.")

YOUNG MEG   Hi. I'm Meg Elliot.

PSEUDOMEG I.   Oh I know. So am I.

YOUNG MEG   And what is your real name, dear?

PSEUDOMEG I   Polly Parrot.

YOUNG MEG   Like the shoes.

PSEUDOMEG I   Oh yes. My father sells them in Boise, so I thought he wouldn't mind me changing my name so much if I named myself after his favorite line of shoes. Oh, Miss Elliot, you're even prettier in person than you are in the movies.

YOUNG MEG   *(Jotting a note.)*   Yes, that's true.   *(She smiles.)*

(Adele laughs.)

PSEUDOMEG I   Omigod, Adele Montrose.

YOUNG ADELE   In the flesh.   *(She and Meg exchange a look.)*

What in the hell is going on here?

YOUNG MEG   It's a Meg Elliot look-alike contest. What does it look like? *(To PseudoMeg I.)*   Thanks a lot, Polly. Could you go over there and wait with the others? Thanks a lot.

PSEUDOMEG I   Oh thank You.   *(She cuts a caper and exits.)*

YOUNG MEG   *(To the wings.)*   Barry, send me the next one. *(Enjoying the exiting figure of Polly.)*   Very nice.   *(Jots a note.)* She's got a better ass than I do.

YOUNG ADELE   So who's sponsoring this contest—you? And I thought I had an ego.

YOUNG MEG   You do.

YOUNG ADELE   I don't look for other little me's to go to bed with.

YOUNG MEG   Luckily for them.

(PseudoMeg II enters.)

PSEUDOMEG II   Oh, I just can't believe it. I can't believe this is really happening to me. Oh, Miss Elliot, I've had a crush on you ever since I saw you in your first picture. You dance just like a dream. Oh and your acting. I cried and cried when you danced off the stage and fell into the orchestra pit and Dick Powell dropped his tuba and ran to you and you just jumped up and started dancing, broken leg and all . . . .

YOUNG MEG   *(Very dryly.)*   They don't make pictures like that anymore.

YOUNG ADELE   *(Quietly but audibly.)*   Thank God.

PSEUDOMEG II   They sure don't. 1931 was a great year for movies. All this stuff that's comin' out since the Production Code is so—so—

YOUNG MEG   Clean.

PSEUDOMEG II   Did you see *Queen Christina*?

(Meg eyes PseudoMeg II with more interest. Adele, alarmed, steps in.)

YOUNG ADELE   *(Mock outrage.)*   That lesbian trash!

YOUNG MEG   *(To PseudoMeg II.)*   Don't mind her. She's from the Virgin Islands. So, honey, what's your name?

PSEUDOMEG II   Julie James. I'm known for my feather act.

YOUNG ADELE   *(Sotto Voce.)*   She does all her acting in the feathers.

YOUNG MEG   *(To PseudoMeg II.)*   I'll keep that in mind.   *(Jots a note.)*   Thank you, Julie. Could you go stand with the other girls?

PSEUDOMEG II   *(Lowering her voice.)*   Wouldn't you like my phone number?

YOUNG ADELE   That's all right, dear. She already has your number.

PSEUDOMEG II   Oh good, because   *(To Meg.)*   I know I've got yours. *(And with this sultry remark, she exits with a wink over her shoulder for Meg.)*

YOUNG MEG   *(Calls out.)*   Barry, is there anyone else or did we do them all?

YOUNG ADELE   You've "done" them all? My aren't you the fast operator.

YOUNG MEG   *(Ignoring Adele, watches/listens to Barry.)*   There are how many more? Twenty? God. Mom always told me when they made me they broke the mold. I guess she was wrong.

YOUNG ADELE   I have to see you.

YOUNG MEG   *(Still calling into the wings.)*   Barry, call the studio. Tell them I've decided to use All of these lovely ladies in that musical number. Why have one of me when you can have forty?

YOUNG ADELE   I'd settle for one of you.

YOUNG MEG   *(To Barry.)*   We'll do a big chorus number. Something real Ziegfeld. Tell them to call Busby Berkeley. He'll know what to do with them. Thank you, girls! You're all very lovely. You all win.   *(Squealing from offstage.)*

YOUNG ADELE   You're the lovely one. Those women are such pale imitations it's pathetic. They can dye their hair and fix their noses, but they'll never have what you have. That special wit, that fire . . .

YOUNG MEG   Adele, buzz off.

YOUNG ADELE Goddammit, why haven't you answered my phone calls? I send you lobsters, orchids—nothing! I'm not used to being ignored. I don't like it.

(There's a furious, scowling standoff for a moment then they both break out laughing.)

YOUNG MEG Why you poor thing.

YOUNG ADELE Are you through here?

YOUNG MEG Don't tell me your maid's got the afternoon off.

YOUNG ADELE I sent champagne and caviar to your apartment just in case you might like company.

YOUNG MEG God, how can you eat caviar?

YOUNG ADELE That's not what I intend to eat.

(Long pause as they eye each other.)

YOUNG MEG Well, I guess everyone deserves a second chance. It's the American way.

YOUNG ADELE Take me home.

YOUNG MEG *(Calls out.)* Barry, I'm through for the day. If anyone needs to reach me, I will be busy. Tell them not to even try. *(To Adele.)* I suppose I'm driving.

(Pseudomeg II appears.)

PSEUDOMEG II It was really a thrill meeting you, Miss Elliot. Meg. If you ever need anything—Anything—give me a call.

YOUNG ADELE Buzz off.

YOUNG MEG *(To Pseudomeg II.)* Thank you, dear, but I believe I'm taken.

PSEUDOMEG II *(Eyes Adele.)* Yeah, I'll bet. *(To Meg.)* Give me a call when you get bored. I'll be home tonight. *(She exits.)*

YOUNG ADELE I promise you won't be bored.

YOUNG MEG *(Heat rising.)* Let's go. Now.

(They exit.)

Scene 15

(The 1980s. Adele's hotel suite. Adele is drinking. She ignores a knocking at the door. A moment later, the maid shows Meg in.)

MEG   Hi.

ADELE   If it isn't that "wonderful" Meg Elliot.

MEG   Cut it out, Adele.

ADELE   Can I interest you in   *(A pause to leave her guessing.)* a drink?

MEG   How about orange juice?

ADELE   Oh, my God, not you, too. I suppose you're in some twelve-step program.   *(To maid.)*   Please go out in the yard and squeeze Miss Elliot some orange juice fresh from the tree.

BONITA   But, Miss Montrose, we are not on the island. We are in a hotel room in New-York-City.

ADELE   *(Enunciating just as slowly.)*   I was jo-king.

BONITA   Oh. Excuse me.   *(She turns her back, exits muttering in Spanish.)*

MEG   Don't be such a wife-beater, Adele.

ADELE   She is not my wife.

MEG   You know what I mean. You're frustrated about the play, so you're taking it out on her. Poor soul. She probably adores you.

ADELE   Actually she has a very large husband. My gardener. He's the one she adores. And he hates me for taking her away. They write each other long, teary letters in that language they speak on my island.

MEG   Spanish?

ADELE   Probably.

MEG   You never used to drink alone.

ADELE   *(Glass in hand.)*   It's a skill I picked up as I got older. And God do I feel old tonight.

MEG   You're doing fine, you know. Don't pay attention to that little asshole Sydney. You're the one who's Adele Montrose.

ADELE   I've never been comfortable working in The Theater. I never had the training. I don't trust my voice. No one who started in silents ever does. This is like living my worst nightmare.

MEG   Adele, you're going to step out on that stage opening night and you're going to be terrific. Trust me.

ADELE   Don't patronize me. I am *not* going to be "terrific." I *do* act from the neck up.

MEG   Adele, you're never done anything from the neck up in your life.

ADELE   Don't be nice. I hate it that you're nice. Luckily it's rare.

MEG   If you're as scared and uncomfortable as you say, why didn't you just stay on your island collecting stock dividends and voting Republican? Why are you doing this play?

ADELE   Because people thought I was dead, and I'm not.

Scene 16

(The 1930s. Meg and Adele are in bed.)

YOUNG MEG   You could stay the night this once. How will he know you weren't with a man?

YOUNG ADELE   Because, darling, I never want to spend the entire night with a man and *he* knows it. So *he* would know. *(She starts to leave the bed; Meg kisses her shoulder.)*   No fair.

YOUNG MEG   He won't fire you. You're too valuable. Why do you let him run your life? You're letting him ruin your life and for no reason.

YOUNG ADELE   He's guiding my career.

YOUNG MEG   Bullshit. If he puts you in many more costume pictures, you're not going to have any career left to guide. You should be playing screwball comedy.

YOUNG ADELE   I think I'll leave that to Jean Arthur.

YOUNG MEG   God she's cute.

YOUNG ADELE   Never mind her. Let's keep talking about *me*.

YOUNG MEG   Aren't you sick of playing the Madonna and Queen Elizabeth?

YOUNG ADELE   *(Dressing.)*   And how many more movies are you going to make dancing around in a bowl of fruit? Dearest, those who live in glass houses . . .

YOUNG MEG   You know I just want to make musical comedies for a couple more years for the money. I'll do my real acting in New York. But poor Adele. You want to be a great serious screen actress, so you think you've got to let that old jackoff run your entire life.

YOUNG ADELE   It'll be worth it. You'll see. I'll finally win my Oscar. *(Bends to kiss Meg.)*   Just think how proud you'll be.

YOUNG MEG   I'd rather have you stay the night.

Scene 17

(The 1980s. Adele's hotel suite.)

MEG   You know, I had this really silly notion that it had something to do with me. That you heard I was going to be in this play, and you just couldn't resist. Ah, vanity.

ADELE   Why did you decide to do it?

MEG   It's a good play.

ADELE   And that was all?

MEG   That's no small thing. Think how many horror movies Bette Davis has been reduced to making, because no one's writing *King Lear* for old women.

ADELE   I rather thought—Oh, never mind. Where is Bonita with your orange juice?

MEG   *(Rising.)*   Never mind, Adele. I should get going.

ADELE   Why? You've done your duty; now you can go some place else and have a good time? I suppose you're meeting someone.

MEG   A friend at a bar. That's all.

ADELE   Is it close by or would you like me to call you a cab?

MEG   It's in the Village.

ADELE   *(Dramatic double take.)*   Meg, you're not going to a gay bar.

MEG   It's a bar for lesbians, yes.

ADELE   My God, where do you get the nerve?

MEG   Adele, it's no big deal anymore. No one cares. I'm not Jane
        Fonda or Mary Tyler Moore. Once in a while I autograph a
        napkin. Would you like to come?

ADELE   I couldn't.

MEG   Oh, come on. What have you got to lose?

ADELE   I may have one foot in the grave, but I am not setting the
        other one in a lesbian bar.

MEG   There are so many women, there's such a variety, you'd just
        be amazed. Women in business suits, faded flannel shirts,
        bikers in leather. It's like a garden.

ADELE   It's not like I'm a lesbian.

MEG   For Christ's sake, Adele, just because you were married
        doesn't mean you're straight.

ADELE   I'm not anything. Not anymore. I think that—at our
        age—it is much more becoming to be celibate.

MEG   Bullshit.

ADELE   You never did have my control.

MEG   I never wanted your control. Not that you were all that
        "controlled." Some of the things we did together I never did
        with anyone else.

(Moment.)

ADELE   Yes.

MEG   Celibate. Jesus, what a waste.

ADELE   *(Moving away.)*   So are you meeting your lover?

MEG   She's a friend.

ADELE   And how old is this friend? Eighteen? Twenty? Did she
        grow up on your movies on the late, late show? Are you her

grandmother's favorite actress? Perhaps you should date her grandmother.

MEG   Adele, I'm going. Sober up before tomorrow. We've got a lot of work to do.

ADELE   The least you could do is be with someone your own age.

MEG   Well, I've been cruising the cemeteries but no luck so far.

ADELE   Maybe you're just not looking in the right place.

(Moment.)

MEG   Adele, in the morning you'd claim you were drunk. And you are. And I guess I'm a gentleman after all. Goodnight, kiddo. You drink the orange juice.   *(She exits.)*

ADELE   She's always walking out on me.   *(Throws a pillow.)*   Why are you *always* walking out on me?!

INTERMISSION

ACT II

Scene 1

(The 1930s. Meg is in a hotel room in New York City. She's in her robe. There's a knock.)

YOUNG MEG Who is it?

YOUNG ADELE *(From offstage.)* Room service.

YOUNG MEG You've got the wrong room.

YOUNG ADELE *(Opens the door, sweeps in.)* My God, don't you ever lock your door? You're not in Michigan anymore.

YOUNG MEG *(Leaps.)* Adele! I can't believe it. I thought you had back-to-back pictures and couldn't come.

YOUNG ADELE We had a little problem with Mr. Barrymore, and they postponed the picture. So here I am. After three glorious days on the Twentieth Century.

YOUNG MEG But you hate long train rides.

YOUNG ADELE I loathe them.

YOUNG MEG Then what are you doing in Manhattan?

YOUNG ADELE What are you doing in Manhattan? Good God, I've never had to come this far for a date in my life. *(Brief pause.)* Meg, I came for your opening night.

(They look at each other.)

YOUNG MEG You really did that?

YOUNG ADELE I know how much The Theater means to you. I should. It's one of your favorite topics. You even went on suspension from the studio so you could do this O'Brien play.

YOUNG MEG O'Neill.

YOUNG ADELE Oh, shut up.

(They kiss.)

YOUNG MEG   I've missed you.

YOUNG ADELE   I suppose the studio will survive, but how the hell did you think I was going to get along without you for four months? You must be mad.

YOUNG MEG   No, just crazy about you.

(They embrace.)

YOUNG MEG   You have too many clothes on.

YOUNG ADELE   Lock your door.

YOUNG MEG   I lie awake nights touching myself, pretending it's you.

YOUNG ADELE   Actually I'm rather glad to hear that. I'd heard you were seeing some Negro singer up in Harlem. Alberta or Ethel Something.

YOUNG MEG   Is that why you're here? I should've known. You didn't miss me at all. Not really.   *(Tickled.)*   You're just jealous.

YOUNG ADELE   Are you?

YOUNG MEG   Have you stayed away from   *(Mocking Vera's voice.)* Vera while I've been gone?

YOUNG ADELE   *(Manages to meet Meg's eyes, but just barely.)*   I've been a veritable saint.

YOUNG MEG   I'll bet. You let her do all the dirty work. It's mean, really, the way you keep her hanging on when you know I'm the one you want.

YOUNG ADELE   Go to hell.

YOUNG MEG   It's true.   *(Smiles, moving closer.)*

YOUNG ADELE   Well, don't gloat about it.

YOUNG MEG   Wanna go up to Harlem tonight after the show and hear them sing?

YOUNG ADELE   *(Hands on Meg's robe.)*   We've got other plans.

YOUNG MEG   *(Hands on Adele's clothes.)*   Darling, why so many buttons? I have to leave for the theater in an hour.   *(Checks a watch/clock.)*   Oops, forty-five minutes.

YOUNG ADELE   What! After I've come all this way?   *(Meg is kissing her; working at her buttons.)*   You are simply outrageous. I have never chased a woman in my life—

YOUNG MEG   You chased me.

YOUNG ADELE   Shut up. And here I am, after travelling through every hick town in America, here I am—   *(Meg kisses her neck.)*   Stop that—vulnerable, and in need, and you're leaving me. Again.

YOUNG MEG   Shhh, Adele. We have forty-five minutes.   *(She kisses her as Adele begins to slip Meg's robe off her shoulders.)*

Scene 2

(The 1980s. A bar. Disco music is in the background. Meg is standing, leaning on a high table, drink in hand. She's been watching the previous scene in her memory. A young woman approaches her.)

JILLY   Care for a drink?

(Meg holds up her drink to indicate she has one.)

JILLY   Waiting for somebody?

MEG   Yes.

JILLY   *(The undaunted butch.)*   Mind if I hang out with you till she comes?

MEG   Oh, she's not coming here. I'm just waiting for her.

JILLY   Oh. Yeah. I've had a couple like that myself. So. Do you just save it all hopin' or you fool around sometimes?

MEG   My you're blunt. Don't you think I'm a little old?

JILLY   Do you?   *(Pause.)*

MEG   I guess tonight yes I do.

JILLY   There's nothin' wrong with doin' a gal who's been around. I wouldn't have to teach you nothin'. Hell, You can prob'ly show me a few things, a little technique. You don't have arthritis, do ya?

MEG   No, but it's awfully late . . .

JILLY   We're both still up. I don't live far. I share a place, but I got my own room.

MEG   What's your name?

JILLY   Jilly.

MEG   You know, Jilly, it's tempting. It is tempting. But . . .

JILLY   Forget the buts. You don't forget the buts, you could be a virgin your whole life.

MEG   But . . .

JILLY   Forget that, too, whatever's got you down, at least for tonight. I don't wanna go home alone either.

MEG   Am I your last chance?

(Jilly doesn't say anything. It's too close to the truth.)

MEG   *(Points.)*   Did you try her?

JILLY   *(Shivers.)*   Have you seen her girlfriend?

MEG   Safety first.

JILLY   *(Empties her glass for courage.)*   Come on.

MEG   Do you have any idea how old I am?

JILLY   What's the difference?   *(Extends her hand.)*

(Just as their hands touch, a woman approaches Meg with a napkin and a pen.)

FAN   It's really you, isn't it?

MEG   I suppose.   *(She accepts the pen and napkin, leans on the table to scribble her autograph.)*

FAN   I'd heard you were "funny," but I thought it was too good to be true.

JILLY   *(To Meg.)*   What's she talkin' about?

FAN   You mean you don't know who she is?

JILLY   A pretty lady at a bar; what's to know?

FAN   Are you coming on to her? You're coming on to Meg Elliot?

JILLY   Who?

MEG   I think that's my cue to leave.

JILLY   Hey, where you goin'? Come on, don't go. You gotta meet my cat.

(Meg has to laugh.)

FAN   Omigod, you mean you still—

MEG   Do I still what? Do I still "date"? Do I still "do it"? Do I still fuck?

FAN   I mean it's great, but—

MEG   Yes, I still fuck. Every chance I get. Whenever I can get away from the nursing home.

JILLY   *(To Fan.)*   Who's Meg Elliot?

FAN   *(To Jilly.)*   Don't you have a VCR?!

JILLY   WHO IS MEG ELLIOT?

MEG   I am. Now let's go see your pussy.

(Fan gasps.)

JILLY   All RIGHT!

MEG   I mean your cat.   *(Jilly and Meg begin to exit.)*

FAN   But is it true about Adele Montrose?

MEG   You'd have to ask her.

(Meg and Jilly exit.)

Scene 3

(The 1930s. A hotel elevator. Adele, in an evening gown, is in the arms of Ramon Riviera who is in a tuxedo. Meg and Mike, also dressed to the nines, are arm in arm. An elevator operator mimes the actions of her job.)

YOUNG ADELE   Oh, Ramon, you devil. Wait till we get upstairs.

MIKE   That movie stunk.

YOUNG MEG   Why we seem to be getting off at the same floor. Isn't that a coincidence?

(They all step off the elevator and wave goodbye to the elevator operator who mimes closing the doors. The hall is empty except for them. It's obviously late. Adele and Ramon kiss, and Mike and Meg kiss. Then Mike kisses Adele and Ramon kisses Meg. Finally—deeply— Mike and Ramon kiss, and Adele and Meg kiss. Then they start off in opposite directions, arm in arm, boy/boy, girl/girl.)

RAMON   Ta ta, girls.

YOUNG ADELE   *(Over her shoulder.)*   Don't scream too much, Ramon. Some people in this hotel may be trying to sleep.

RAMON   That's their problem, dearie.

YOUNG MEG   Sleep sure isn't what's on *my* mind.   *(Long eye contact with Adele.)*   Hi.

YOUNG ADELE   Good-bye, boys.

(We fade as the two couples go their own ways.)

Scene 4

(The 1980s. It's rehearsal, the morning after. Adele's maid is massaging her neck, etc. Meg, head on her arms, looking quite worn, is nursing a coffee and a hangover.)

ADELE   Late night?

MEG   *(Mumbles.)*   Yes.

ADELE   Did you have a nice time?

MEG   *(Mumbles.)*   Yes.

ADELE   Did you lose your vocabulary?

MEG   *(Head rises.)*   My vocabulary? Oh yes, I seem to.   *(Head sinks back onto arms.)*

(Silence.)

ADELE   Well?!

MEG   You mean I can talk in front of this maid?

ADELE   She doesn't speak the language that well.

(Bonita winks. Meg smiles.)

ADELE   *(Doesn't catch the wink but senses something.)*   But no, I'd rather you didn't.

MEG   Doesn't it get awfully stifling in that closet, Adele?

ADELE   They're right. They're All right. All the columnists. All the people who've said I hate you. I do hate you. Through and through.   *(She punctuates her points by slamming her hand down on the table, causing Meg and her hangover great discomfort. Brief pause then.)*   How young was she?

MEG   Twenty-three.

ADELE   But a very mature twenty-three, I'm sure.

MEG   She'd never heard of me. Someone at the bar who knows me from her VCR told her. It was actually rather funny.

ADELE   Are you going to see her again?

MEG   It probably isn't a good idea.

ADELE   But are you?

MEG   When I'm with someone that much younger I dread the daylight almost as much as you used to. It makes me sad. No, I won't see her again.   *(Indicates Bonita.)*   May I borrow her fingers for a few minutes? Bonita, I would be your slave if you would massage my neck for a couple of minutes.

BONITA   Of course, Miss Elliot.   *(Bonita hesitates.)*   Here?   *(Massages.)*

MEG   Oh yes.   *(Moans with delight.)*

ADELE   *(Meg's moans are getting to her, but she talks on.)*   Here comes Clyde. He's perspiring. I wonder what I've done wrong now.

MEG   Pretend you can't hear him. Better yet, *don't* hear him. All the time he's talking to you, just picture him having sex with a goat.

ADELE   You would put it in terms of sex. One good fuck and that's all you can think about. *(Exploding.)* How could you do something so intimate with someone you barely know?

MEG   Practice. Look, Queen Elizabeth, you slept with plenty of strange pussy in your day.

(Bonita laughs, then catches herself and tries to stifle the laugh.)

ADELE   *(To Bonita.)* She means cats, Bonita. *(Thinks of the word but mispronounces it as* gay toes.*)* Gatos. I used to own several rare Persian gatos, and some nights I would let them sleep on my bed.

MEG   Adele, nobody cares.

ADELE   If I was lonely, I would sometimes let Vera curl up with me. I didn't let just any old alley cat share my bed.

MEG   Good old Vera. What finally killed her?

ADELE   One too many Disney pictures.

BONITA   *(To Meg.)* Let me get you some more coffee.

MEG   You're such a dear. She doesn't deserve you.

ADELE   *(To Bonita as Bonita is exiting.)* I could use some, too.

BONITA   Yes, señora. *(Exits, grumbling barely under her breath in Spanish.)*

ADELE   Dear Vera. I do miss her. She should have been the great love of my life. I always felt guilty that she wasn't.

SYDNEY   *(Enters talking.)* All right, let's get this rehearsal under way. *(To offstage.)* Clyde, whatever it is you're trying to say is going to have to wait until after lunch. Places. *(As Meg and Adele show no sign of budging.)* Please?

Scene 5

(The 1930s and 1980s. Rehearsal. At the studio, in the 1930s, Ramon and Adele are doing a scene, and so are Meg and Mike. At the theater, in the 1980s, Meg and Adele are also acting their hearts out.)

YOUNG ADELE   *(In costume dress.)* I thought our love meant the world to you, Pierre. Oh, Pierre, Pierre, if I mean no more to

you than this I shall return to the convent and take my
final vows.

RAMON   No!

YOUNG ADELE   Yes!

RAMON   Never!   *(Sweeps Adele into his arms.)*

YOUNG MEG   But you can't give up dancin'! Dancin' is your life!

MIKE   But, babe, I gotta. If I don't hit the books, I'll never get into
medical school, an' it'll break my poor mother's heart.

YOUNG MEG   But if you give up the stage, you'll break your *own*
heart. Dancin', singin', they're like bread and butter to kids
like you'n me.

MIKE   But will Mom ever understand? Can she ever forgive me?

YOUNG MEG   Forgive you?! She'll thank you! When she sees you on
Broadway, when she hears those crowds cheer, she'll be your
biggest fan!

(Mike and Meg do a quick dance step into each other's arms)

ADELE   They want to put us in a nursing home. Sister, they want
to put us away.

MEG   *(Pouting, crying.)*   Oh, don't let them, sissy. Sissy, don't let
them. I don't want to go. I want to stay here.   *(She breaks
character.)*   God, I sound like an ancient Shirley Temple. All I
need is Rochelle Hudson.

ADELE   I believe that's me.

SYDNEY   Well, it sounds marvelous.

MEG   Where's Clyde? I want to talk to him about this speech.

SYDNEY   Another rewrite?!

ADELE   I may not deliver the lines well, but at least I deliver them
as written.

SYDNEY   Oh God, we open in three days.

MEG   Sydney, where is Clyde?

ADELE   Out hiring a hitman.   *(Gives Meg a pointed look.)*

MEG   Adele, butt out.

ADELE   I suppose you argue about your lines constantly because you are a serious artiste.

MEG   I care. Is that a crime?

ADELE   You always did look down on my approach to acting.

MEG   You approach acting through your checkbook.

SYDNEY   Meg, we can talk to Clyde about that line later.

MEG   Where is he? Why isn't he here? If he didn't want to work with us, why in the hell did he insist on casting us?

ADELE   Temporary insanity.

MEG   Sydney, we really should be getting some work done.

SYDNEY   You two make me crazy. Crazy!   *(Sydney stalks away, exits.)*

(Adele and Meg look at each other.)

MEG   What's she/he so mad about?

ADELE   It's beyond me.

MEG   I didn't mean that about your checkbook.

ADELE   I Was nominated for an Oscar, you know.

MEG   Yes. I remember.

ADELE   Of course, you were nominated five times.

MEG   But who's counting.

ADELE   I did.

Scene 6

(The 1930s. Meg's apartment.)

YOUNG ADELE   I can't believe I got the nomination.

YOUNG MEG   Congratulations.

YOUNG ADELE   Finally. After all these years. And you were nominated, too. Isn't that wonderful?

YOUNG MEG   I just hope neither of us win.

YOUNG ADELE   What?! *(Brief pause.)* Oh, that's true. That would be hard.

YOUNG MEG   I bet that new Capra film sweeps the Awards.

YOUNG ADELE   It's possible.

YOUNG MEG   You really wanna win, don't you?

YOUNG ADELE   yes.

YOUNG MEG   Hey, want me to be your date? I'll wear a tux. I look really cute in a tux. I wore one last fall when I was at that party in Paris.

YOUNG ADELE   God, you were lucky that never made the papers.

YOUNG MEG   The French are much more relaxed about lesbianism. It wasn't news to them.

YOUNG ADELE   It would've been if they'd known you were a famous American movie star.

YOUNG MEG   Of course, they knew. My fame is international.

YOUNG ADELE   It was still a risk.

YOUNG MEG   Well, it was worth it, Adele. Some things are.

YOUNG ADELE   Are we out of cigarettes?

YOUNG MEG   I love it when you say "we," like we're a couple.

YOUNG ADELE   We Are a couple.

YOUNG MEG   Then why don't we go on dates?

YOUNG ADELE   We *go* on dates.

YOUNG MEG   Sure. With Mike and Ramon. Me with Mike. You with Ramon. Then we switch dates at the hotel, and you and I fuck each other's brains out in one room while they do something involving a grapefruit in another. That is Not dating.

YOUNG ADELE   I won't go to the Academy Awards with you. I will say hello.

YOUNG MEG   Oh thank you.

YOUNG ADELE   Don't be mad.

YOUNG MEG   Do you love me at all?

YOUNG ADELE   Utterly. And absolutely.

YOUNG MEG   Even if I win?

YOUNG ADELE   Go to hell.

YOUNG MEG   Even if I wear a tuxedo to the Academy Awards?

YOUNG ADELE   You wouldn't. Would you?

YOUNG MEG   Sure. Why not? Marlene wore one in *Morocco* and people ate it up.

YOUNG ADELE   Please don't.

YOUNG MEG   Would you stop seeing me if I did? Me, the great love of your life?

YOUNG ADELE   He knows about us. And he said if there's ever a breath of scandal, he'll wrap himself in the bosom of the Baptist Church and ruin us both.

YOUNG MEG   Fuck him.

YOUNG ADELE   I have. When I was a kid. That's how I got my first part.

(Silence. Finally.)

YOUNG MEG   You really slept with him?

YOUNG ADELE   Believe me, I tried to sleep through it.

YOUNG MEG   That evil son-of-a-bitch.

YOUNG ADELE   It was a long time ago.

YOUNG MEG   How old were you?

YOUNG ADELE   Young.

YOUNG MEG   Adele, how can you live this way?

YOUNG ADELE Meg, what do you want? Do you want me to invite Louella over for an intimate dinner at home with me and the missus? Don't be ridiculous.

YOUNG MEG Look, I'm not asking to walk down Sunset Boulevard holding your hand. Though God knows I wish I could. I wish I could. I just want— *(She stops, on the verge of tears, searching for the words.)* I just want to know I mean more to you than your career. Do I?

YOUNG ADELE How can you ask that?

YOUNG MEG Why don't you answer?

YOUNG ADELE I was in such a good mood, why must you ruin it? I've been nominated for an Oscar! Do you know how many years I've waited for this day? I have a wonderful lover and a wonderful career. You both mean so much to me, why must I choose?

YOUNG MEG Because I'm afraid one of these days you'll feel you have to, and I'll be out the door.

YOUNG ADELE Don't be silly.

(Meg pulls away from Adele.)

Scene 7

(The 1980s. On one side of the stage is a TV studio where Loren Gerard is interviewing Meg. On the other side of the stage, Adele sits in the dark watching the blue light of the television set, drinking.)

LOREN GERARD Miss Elliot, welcome to *Nightlife*.

MEG Thank you, Loren.

LOREN Tomorrow night's the big night.

MEG It certainly is.

LOREN We were terribly sorry your illustrious co-star couldn't make it. I hope that doesn't mean you two still aren't—how can we word this delicately?—

MEG I'm sure you can't.

LOREN Overly fond of each other.

MEG   Oh, Loren, don't be silly. Adele and I are incredibly fond of each other. We always have been.

ADELE   *(To the screen.)*   Pushing it. You are always pushing it. *(She takes a drink.)*

LOREN   Oh darling, come clean. Everyone knows you despise each other.

MEG   Let's talk about the play.

(Lights dim on this interview though it continues, and the action moves to an interview in the 1930s. The younger Adele enters in her Oscar finery, pursued by a reporter with a 1930s radio microphone.)

REPORTER   Adele! Adele Montrose. Adele, tell us the truth. What will make you happier—winning the Academy Award or getting to attend the ceremony with Ramon Riviera?

YOUNG ADELE   *(Leaning into the mike, all warmth and charm.)*   Well, of course, my fans know how much Ramon means to me. But he's not the only man in my life.

REPORTER   Adele! My heavens!

YOUNG ADELE   I mean Oscar.

REPORTER   *(Into the mike.)*   Oh my, aren't we relieved?

YOUNG ADELE   I'm sure Ramon would be willing to share me with that little gold man waiting inside. And I hope all my fans out there in radioland have their fingers crossed for me.

REPORTER   Oh, I'm sure they do, Adele, I'm sure they do. *(He/she spots young Meg.)*   And here comes that very special nominee, Meg Elliot. Meg, Meg, over here!

YOUNG MEG   *(To Adele.)*   Nice dress.

YOUNG ADELE   Thank you.

REPORTER   How sweet. You two do know each other.

YOUNG ADELE   Yes, of course. Meg, it's so good to see you.

YOUNG MEG   Likewise. *(To the reporter and the folks in radioland.)*   So I hear Adele's got it in the bag. I don't know what you wanna talk to me for.

REPORTER   Oh, Meg, you're always so funny.

YOUNG MEG   You couldn't get Barbara Stanwyck, so you had to settle for me?

REPORTER   I'm sure half the men in America would be glad to "settle" for you, Meg Elliot.

YOUNG MEG   Well, they don't interest me.

(Young Adele looks physically ill.)

YOUNG MEG   Nope. As soon as we get this little show over with, I'm going into the nunnery.

REPORTER   Why, Meg, I never knew you were Catholic.

YOUNG MEG   I'm not. But I hope they don't hold that against me.

REPORTER   But now seriously, Meg, aren't you terribly excited about this Oscar nomination?

YOUNG MEG   Oh sure.   *(The reporter waits for more. Meg looks at him/her.)*

YOUNG MEG   Oh, you want me to bubble on about it. Of course, I'm happy. Just being nominated is such an honor, just being in the company of great actresses like Greta Garbo and Adele Montrose is enough for me.

REPORTER   *(Taken aback.)*   You mean you don't care if you win?

YOUNG MEG   Nope. I put my trust in God and the Academy. Don't you, Adele?

YOUNG ADELE   Ah well, why yes.

YOUNG MEG   When you love what you do and love and respect your fellow actresses, winning awards is just icing on the cake. I can take it or leave it.

YOUNG ADELE   Of course, I'd rather take it.

REPORTER   Oh I just wish you both could win.

YOUNG MEG   So do I.

(Young Adele and Young Meg exit waving to their fans. Reporter exits with his/her microphone. Lights rise on the 1980s interview where the fur is flying.)

MEG   Well, what's that got to do with anything?

LOREN   I just thought—

MEG   I doubt that.

LOREN   I just love how feisty you are, even at your advanced age.

MEG   And how old are you, Loren?

ADELE   *(To her TV set.)*   Careful, Meg.

LOREN   Well, I—

MEG   You know, I've never seen a plastic surgeon in my life. I bet you wish you could say the same.

LOREN   And now a word from our sponsors. *(A fake smile disappears as the light on the camera goes off.)*   You rotten old bitch! I've got half a mind—

MEG   How true.

LOREN   I should come back from commercial and tell them all I know about you.

MEG   Fine.

LOREN   What?! Obviously you don't know what I'm getting at.

MEG   Of course, I know what you're getting at. Go on. Tell.

(Loren is dumbfounded.)

MEG   No. Really. Go ahead.   *(Sits patiently, waiting.)*

LOREN   What's the catch?

MEG   No catch.

LOREN   *(Big realization.)*   You know about me, is that it?

MEG   Why no, Loren, I didn't.   *(Meg gives him/her a piercing look.)* My.

LOREN   Shit.   *(To a person offstage.)*   Bob, that is the end of the interview. Cut to that segment we weren't going to use; the one about Doris Day's dogs.

MEG   *(Rising.)*   No guts, no glory.

LOREN   *(Suddenly vulnerable.)*   Please don't tell anyone.

MEG   Of course not.   *(She reaches for Loren's hand; shakes it.)*   I hope you're coming to the opening.

LOREN   *(Sincerely relieved.)*   Well, of course. I wouldn't miss it.

MEG   *(Pausing on her way out.)*   It's not a great way to spend your life, Loren. Hiding. Pretend dating. Pretend marriages. Living a lie. Living in fear. Especially when you only get the one life.

(Pause.)

LOREN   I can't.

MEG   I know.   *(She exits.)*

(After a moment, the lights lower on Loren, but Adele is still watching her TV. The commercial is still on but almost over.)

ADELE   *(Talking to the TV.)*   Michael, you were the best hoofer Meg ever danced with. Why in the hell are you selling dogfood? The least you could do is advertise a nice gourmet coffee. *(Frowns as Doris and her dogs appear.)*   Oh my God, Doris Day. Look at that hair. But where's Meg? What happened to Meg? *(Brief pause.)*   She scared you, too, didn't she?

Scene 8

(The 1930s. The ladies room at the Oscars. Adele is at the mirror. Meg enters.)

YOUNG MEG   Hi.

YOUNG ADELE   *(Very formal.)*   Oh, why hello.

YOUNG MEG   Is somebody in here besides us?

YOUNG ADELE   No, they're all out there. I guess they must care who the best supporting actress is.

YOUNG MEG   We're actually alone?

YOUNG ADELE   I just said so.

YOUNG MEG   Then let me kiss you for luck.

YOUNG ADELE   Have you lost your mind?   *(Pause.)*

YOUNG MEG It's just that I miss you.

YOUNG ADELE *(Lowering her voice.)* I'll see you later. After. Now go away.

YOUNG MEG You look beautiful.

YOUNG ADELE *(To the mirror.)* Yes.

YOUNG MEG Adele . . . *(She thinks better of saying it.)*

YOUNG ADELE What?

YOUNG MEG Never mind.

YOUNG ADELE I'm afraid.

YOUNG MEG I know. So am I.

YOUNG ADELE Please go away. I need to finish my face.

YOUNG MEG I love you, Adele.

YOUNG ADELE Not here.

(Meg looks at Adele for a moment then exits. After another moment, Adele returns to sculpting her eyebrows.)

Scene 9

(The 1980s. Opening night. Adele is at the mirror sculpting her face. Meg is gargling, spits.)

ADELE You're still so delicate, so refined. It's done my heart good to know you've never changed.

MEG *(Looking at Adele's face in the mirror.)* I feel so sorry for your skin. Why don't you just get one of those spray guns like they use to paint houses?

ADELE Shouldn't you be getting into your costume?

MEG What's the rush? Curtain doesn't go up for half an hour.

ADELE You never did like to put your clothes on.

(They look at each other. Sydney pops in.)

SYDNEY   Twenty-eight minutes to curtain, ladies. Need any help? Buttons buttoned or anything?

ADELE   I think we can manage, thank you.

SYDNEY   Now don't be nervous.

ADELE   Why should we be nervous? We know our lines.

SYDNEY   Did anybody tell you Kate Hepburn is out there?

ADELE   Most people would worry that telling us something like that might make us nervous.

SYDNEY   So you'd rather not know about Ron and Nancy?

MEG   Oh God, who invited them?   *(Glares at Adele.)*

ADELE   Don't look at me. I have Some taste.

SYDNEY   Don't forget to speak up. That's a big theater out there.

MEG   Sydney, I'm about to take off my brassiere and swing it whooping over my head. It's an old ritual of mine. You shouldn't be in here.

SYDNEY   I'm gone. Twenty-six minutes to curtain.   *(Exits.)*

MEG   Sydney's terrified we're going to forget our lines or pee our pants on stage.

ADELE   She's/He's afraid one of us is going to drop dead.

MEG   It's certainly a possibility.

ADELE   *(Finishing her face.)*   Oh, never mind her/him. There. I'm ravishing.   *(Pause. She leans back, away from the mirror, squints.)* If you're sitting in the balcony.   *(Pause.)*   The second balcony.

MEG   I still say you look better without all that crap.

ADELE   *(With finality.)*   Well, I need it.

MEG   You always did have to have something—or someone—to hide behind.

ADELE   Michael's doing dogfood commercials.

MEG   Ramon's been dead for years. He didn't keep very nice company, especially the older he got.

ADELE   He was killed by some boy he picked up, wasn't he?

MEG   So you did keep in touch, even on your island.

ADELE   Actually I was quite lonely. *(An exchanged glance.)*   What?

MEG   We still stir something in each other.

ADELE   Nonsense.

MEG   Just because you were married all those years doesn't make you straight. I bet you only had sex with him once a year—every New Year's Eve like clockwork.

ADELE   Don't you ever get tired of talking about sex?

MEG   I get tired of talking.

(Moment.)

ADELE   Christ, we're playing sisters in this play. What strange chemistry there's going to be.

MEG   Incest is best.

ADELE   How did you ever survive in Hollywood as long as you did the way you talk?

MEG   Sometimes Hollywood protects its own. Especially if they love you. And for some reason they loved me. Maybe it was because I said all the things other people wanted to but didn't have the guts.

ADELE   You're buttoning that wrong. *(The buttons on Meg's housedress are off a button.)*   Here. Unless you want me to call Sydney.

MEG   God forbid. *(She's a little unsettled that she buttoned it wrong, but she also enjoys being so close to Adele.)*

ADELE   I guess we're both nervous.

MEG   Nervous? Who me? All of New York is out there just waiting to tell the country what Meg Elliot and Adele Montrose look like now they're on Medicare. Is it true they can't stand the sight of each other? Is that really them? Hell, I can't wait.

ADELE   We should have done this years ago, while we were young, before we became a sideshow at the circus.

MEG   Do you ever wonder?

ADELE   What?

MEG   Do you ever wish we were young again? Young now? Young together?

ADELE   I could never live through that twice. Especially that parting.

MEG   So many more people are out of the closet today. Being gay, being a lesbian isn't so utterly hidden, so shameful. My God, we have our own parades. If we'd been together now, we could have been more honest without risking everything. Maybe without so much pressure we might have stayed together.

ADELE   Oh Meg, for heaven's sake, pressure? There's just as much pressure to stay hidden in Hollywood as there ever was. Name me three living movie stars who are openly gay. Name me one.

(Pause.)

MEG   You're right.

ADELE   I'm sorry. I'm sorry I'm right.

MEG   I was trying to kid myself and you brought me right back to earth. You're right. Being young today wouldn't solve anything. We'd still be apart.

ADELE   You'd probably be in Canada homesteading.

MEG   Nope. I'd still be in Hollywood, but I'd be doing sitcoms, crying all the way to the bank about how much I'd rather be doing theater. And you, Adele. You'd still be trying to please the boys, so they'd let you have one, pretty please just one of the Meryl Streep parts so you could win your Oscar.

ADELE   But you won the Oscar.

MEG   Yes, I did.

Scene 10

(The 1930s. A bed. Adele is in it with a man.)

MAN   I can't believe what just happened. Jesus. Adele Montrose.

YOUNG ADELE   Don't tell me this was your first celebrity fuck.

MAN   Uh huh. Jesus, I still can't believe it.

YOUNG ADELE   Neither can I.

MAN   It was really great. Was it great for you?

YOUNG ADELE   Great?

MAN   Well, okay?

YOUNG ADELE   Why must men always get a scorecard? I laid here and let you do it. You messed up my sheets. What more do you want?

MAN   To do it again?

YOUNG ADELE   You're joking.

MAN   Come on. It'll make you feel better. I mean, I know you missed out on winning an Oscar tonight. Must be rough. I was right there, right outside where the ceremony was. You looked so elegant going in. You kinda glided, just like a queen. And here I am lyin' right next to you, Adele Montrose. I still can't believe it.

YOUNG ADELE   Go home.

MAN   Aw, come on. I'll do it better this time. I know I kinda jumped the gun—

YOUNG ADELE   Go home. Cut a notch in your bedpost. Tell your friends. And pull the door closed behind you.

MAN   All you gotta do is touch it—

YOUNG ADELE   Listen, asshole, if you aren't out of this bed and out of my house in sixty seconds my maid is going to come in here and shoot you. So get out!

(The man leaps out of bed wearing the sheet. He grabs his clothes as Meg enters.)

MAN   Jesus! You don't have to shoot me, I'm gone.   *(Still wearing Adele's sheet, clutching his clothes, he runs out.)*

(Meg has just been looking at Adele. Finally, she bends and picks up a tie. She dangles it from two fingers.)

YOUNG MEG He's not moving too fast in your sheet. Should I try to catch him with this, or will he be back?

YOUNG ADELE Throw it in the wastebasket. Over there. *(Points.)*

YOUNG MEG Thank you. After all, I've never been here before, so I don't know where things are. Nice any stranger you pick up off the street gets to come here and I don't.

YOUNG ADELE And you shouldn't be here now.

YOUNG MEG Do you do this often? You always feed me such a bunch of baloney about why I can't come to your house, but you probably just don't want me checking the sheets for pecker tracks.

YOUNG ADELE Don't make a big thing out of this. I was depressed, and he was handy. You were with that guy who looks like Bill Powell, the one who's supposed to be hung like a horse.

YOUNG MEG Yes, and I ditched him right after the ceremony and went home to wait for you. Like I was supposed to.

YOUNG ADELE Well, I just wasn't in the mood to help you celebrate, love. Maybe I'll be more adult next time.

YOUNG MEG I'm not going to let you make me feel sorry I won.

YOUNG ADELE Well, that's all I feel like doing just now, so why did you come?

YOUNG MEG I feel so stupid. I was concerned. And lonely. Isn't that dumb? God is that stupid.

YOUNG ADELE Look, I'm sorry you walked in on that. Another thirty seconds and he would have been gone and you would have been none the wiser.

YOUNG MEG Yes, that's true. I would have been none the wiser.

YOUNG ADELE You're always so disappointed in me. You always expect more of me than I can give. You always think I'm someone I'm not. What I am is a decent but obviously not outstanding movie actress who cares more about success than anything else in the world, including you. And tonight, all my grovelling, all the money the studio spread around, all of it meant nothing. Not a damn thing. You just breeze in spitting in their faces and they give you the Oscar and a standing ovation.

YOUNG MEG I'm going to go home now, before anything else is said that we can't take back.

YOUNG ADELE Why don't you go get yourself laid? Get that nose out of the air and down into somebody's business.

YOUNG MEG Goddammit! *(She grabs Adele by the shoulders, shakes her.)* You're better than this. *(Her hands remain on Adele.)*

YOUNG ADELE No, I'm not. Only in your fantasy. We're both good at fantasy. It's our business.

YOUNG MEG I love you. That's not fantasy.

YOUNG ADELE Don't.

YOUNG MEG I love you, Adele. *(She kisses Adele. Adele stiffens, tries to pull away, but finally, ravenously, gives in to the kiss. Eventually.)* Come away with me. We need to get away together.

YOUNG ADELE I can't.

YOUNG MEG Why not? Neither of us has a picture scheduled for at least three weeks.

YOUNG ADELE I can't. I'm going to be busy.

YOUNG MEG Doing what?

YOUNG ADELE Eloping.

YOUNG MEG What?!

YOUNG ADELE It won't affect us. It's just a publicity gimmick. He seems like a nice man. He's just down on his luck and needs a job and marrying me is it.

YOUNG MEG The studio arranged this, didn't they?

YOUNG ADELE Yes.

YOUNG MEG But you let them.

YOUNG ADELE Look on the bright side. I won't have to pretend to be dating men anymore. Every so often the fan magazines will drop by to snap a few pictures of my new husband and me "at home" and the rest of the time I'll be free to be with you.

YOUNG MEG   And when the public gets bored with this guy, you'll get a divorce and let the studio find you a new and improved husband. Maybe your playmate from tonight would be interested.

YOUNG ADELE   Pa-leeze.

YOUNG MEG   How can you marry someone you don't even know? Just to please your public and a hypocrite of a studio head who fucks fourteen-year-old girls?

YOUNG ADELE   Meg—

YOUNG MEG   How can you marry someone who isn't me?

YOUNG ADELE   Why must you judge everything I do?

YOUNG MEG   Because I don't want to be ashamed of you. I'm afraid I can't love someone I'm ashamed of.

YOUNG ADELE   But you do. You can't stop yourself. And neither can I. That's why I'm getting married. For us.

YOUNG MEG   Don't tell me that.

YOUNG ADELE   But it's true. If I'm married, we can be together so much easier. The man I'm marrying knows, and he'll just go off to the guest house when you "visit" me. Don't you see how easy it can be?

YOUNG MEG   I don't want it to be "easy."

YOUNG ADELE   Goddammit, why not?

YOUNG MEG   *(Moving to the door.)*   I'm going to go now. I'll try not to wake the maid.

YOUNG ADELE   *(Running to Meg; takes her arm.)*   Please don't. Stay. Please. I'm sorry I didn't come over to help you celebrate. I'm glad you won. You deserved to win.

YOUNG MEG   Let me go, Adele. *(She touches Adele's face with her free hand; kisses her lightly but firmly, then pulls loose.)*   Have a good life. Try not to degrade yourself any more than you absolutely have to. *(She exits.)*

YOUNG ADELE   Meg?! Megan! Please don't . . . I won't . . . Will you stay if I call off . . . Oh God, Meg.

Scene 11

(The 1980s. Opening night. The dressing room.)

ADELE   You were good. That was what hurt so much. You were such a good actress. You weren't acting. You really felt what you said, so you made the audience feel. I just postured.

MEG   That's not true.

ADELE   I probably still do. And you're still a great actress. Something tells me I'm going to be very depressed after the Tony Awards.

MEG   Stop. *(But she's impressed—amazed—that Adele has come so far that she can be dryly humorous on the subject of awards.)*

ADELE   Is my lipstick crooked on this side, do you think?

MEG   *(Moving in closer than she really needs to to check.)*   No, it's fine. All twelve pounds of it.

ADELE   God, I missed you.

MEG   You never called. You never wrote. Never pounded on my door. How could you let me leave?

ADELE   I made a choice.

MEG   Me or your career? But you could have had both! Honest to God, you could have had both.

ADELE   I was afraid.

MEG   Have you ever gotten over it? Being afraid.

ADELE   No. But I'm not dead yet.   *(Moment then Sydney sticks her/his head in.)*

SYDNEY   Twelve minutes, ladies. All set? Got those lines down? Is there anything I can get for you?

ADELE   Out.

SYDNEY   Pardon me?

ADELE   You heard me. Out. Get out. If I see you again before the opening night party, I am personally going to throw you out that window. Get out!

SYDNEY Come on, Adele, don't get testy. I'm just trying to help you.

MEG Get out of here this minute, junior, or neither of us is going on and it will be your fault. You don't talk to stars that way. That audience didn't come to see you, so if you don't want to act this performance yourself you get your motherfucking ass out of here. Get out!

SYDNEY *(Exiting in shock, eyes bulging, hands in the air as if washing her/his hands of it.)* All right. Fine. I don't care. *(Exits.)*

ADELE Thank you.

MEG Thank you.

ADELE That was absolutely brilliant. You should play Lear. You always did like drag.

MEG God, you're gorgeous.

ADELE I would like very much to kiss you, but it would ruin our make-up.

MEG It'll look realistic smudged. We are, after all, playing two doddering old fools.

ADELE I don't feel doddering.

MEG Neither do I.

ADELE You know, I wasn't telling the whole truth when I said why I agreed to do this play. I wanted to see you. I had to see you. I was afraid if I just called or wrote you wouldn't answer. This way you were trapped. You couldn't run away.

MEG I wouldn't have run. Why the hell do you think I agreed to be in this piece of crap in the first place?

ADELE *(Reaches out, strokes Meg's hair.)* I'm so glad there's longevity in my family.

MEG Let's not waste any more time. *(They are moving closer as the curtain falls.)*

CURTAIN

Selected Bibliography

Other Plays and Critical Sources of Interest

Austin, Gayle. *Feminist Theories for Dramatic Criticism*. Ann Arbor: University of Michigan, 1990.

Butler, Audrey. *Radical Perversions: Two Dyke Plays*. Toronto: Women's Press, 1990.

Butler, Judith. *Gender Trouble: Feminism and the Subversion of Identity*. New York: Routledge, 1990.

Case, Sue-Ellen. *Feminism and Theatre*. New York: Methuen, 1988.

_____. *Performing Feminisms: Feminist Critical Theory and Theatre*. Baltimore: Johns Hopkins, 1990.

Chambers, Jane. *My Blue Heaven* (1981), *Last Summer at Bluefish Cove* (1982), *Burning* (1983), *Warrior at Rest* (1984), *Chasin' Jason* (1987), *A Late Snow* (1989). New York: JH Press.

Chinoy, Helen Krich and Linda Walsh Jenkins. *Women in American Theatre*. New York: Theatre Communications Group, 1987.

Crossland, Jackie. *Collateral Damage: The Tragedy of Medea*. Vancouver: Press Gang Publishers, 1992.

Curtin, Kaier. *"We Can Always Call Them Bulgarians": The Emergence of Lesbians and Gay Men on the American Stage*. Boston: Alyson, 1987.

Davis, Jill, ed. *Lesbian Plays*. London: Methuen London Ltd., 1986.

_____, ed. *Lesbian Plays II*. London: Methuen London Ltd., 1989.

Dreher, Sarah. *Lesbian Stages*. Norwich, VT: New Victoria, 1988.

Hart, Lynda. "Canonizing Lesbians?" *Modern American Drama: The Female Canon*, 275-292.

_____, ed. *Making a Spectacle: Feminist Essays on Contemporary Women's Theatre*. Ann Arbor: University of Michigan, 1989.

Malpede, Karen. *Women in Theatre: Compassion & Hope*. Limelight.

McDermott, Kate, ed., *Places, Please! The First Anthology of Lesbian Plays*. San Francisco: Spinsters, 1985.

Munt, Sally, ed. *New Lesbian Criticism: Literary and Cultural Readings*. New York: Columbia University Press, 1992.

Shewey, Don, ed. *Out Front: Contemporary Gay and Lesbian Plays*. New York: Grove, 1988.

Wandor, Michelene. *Carry On, Understudies: Theatre and Sexual Politics*. New York: Routledge, 1986.

Weston, Kath. *Families We Choose: Lesbians, Gays, Kinship*. New York: Columbia University Press, 1991.